Doing Something Different

Doing Something Different

Solution-Focused Brief Therapy Practices

EDITED BY
Thorana S. Nelson

Routledge
Taylor & Francis Group
New York   London

Routledge
Taylor & Francis Group
270 Madison Avenue
New York, NY 10016

Routledge
Taylor & Francis Group
27 Church Road
Hove, East Sussex BN3 2FA

© 2010 by Taylor and Francis Group, LLC
Routledge is an imprint of Taylor & Francis Group, an Informa business

Printed in the United States of America on acid-free paper
10 9 8 7 6 5 4 3 2 1

International Standard Book Number: 978-0-415-87961-3 (Paperback)

Library of Congress Cataloging-in-Publication Data

Doing something different : solution-focused brief therapy practices / Thorana S. Nelson, editor.
    p. cm.
Includes bibliographical references and index.
ISBN 978-0-415-87961-3 (pbk. : alk. paper)
1. Solution-focused brief therapy. I. Nelson, Thorana Strever. II. Title.

RC489.S65D64 2010
616.89'147--dc22   2009053534

Visit the Taylor & Francis Web site at
http://www.taylorandfrancis.com

and the Routledge Web site at
http://www.routledgementalhealth.com

CONTENTS

PART II Training

PART V   Outrageous Moments in Therapy

FOREWORD

My first reaction to the request to write the forward for *Doing Something Different: Solution-Focused Brief Therapy Practices* was that I likely wouldn't have much to say that would be worth saying. I'm inclined to say less rather than more, both in life and when it comes to Solution-Focused Brief Therapy (SFBT). I must admit, I haven't kept up reading all of the new books that have come out about SFBT. I'm still quite focused on the original basic ideas, continuing to be fascinated with how much there is to learn about client wisdom, elegance in practice, simple effectiveness, and having the right tool ready for the right moment and watching it do its job—as one of the short pieces in this book describes about a mate who was a master boat builder.

Then I realized that the contributors to *Doing Something Different* are fellow travelers on this path. Working away with solution-focused ideas and practices. Trying to get better. Sharing their discoveries along the way. I can't say that I would follow all of them into the various nooks and crannies of practice that they have explored. On the other hand, there are some whose experiments will stick with me and undoubtedly show up in one of my therapy sessions or training events in the weeks to come. One of the things I have been most thankful for in finding solution-focused brief therapy along the way is how our worldwide community rises to an occasion such as the early beginnings of this book, and gives so freely of their time and experience for the good of us all and for the good of our model.

I acquired a phrase from Harry Korman during his plenary presentation at the Solution-Focused Brief Therapy Association (SFBTA) conference in Denver, Colorado in 2004. "From how you know yourself [that's Harry's piece]…what would you say you are most likely to do under these circumstances to try making things better?" Since Denver, this phrase crops up regularly in my sessions. At my stage of practice and learning, these gems are very much appreciated—like a tiny jack-knife given to me by a special friend years ago. Every time I fish it out of my pocket to open mail or do a quick repair on something, I'm glad it's there.

There are many such treasures in this book. Enjoy the hunt.

Lance Taylor
President, Solution-Focused Brief Therapy Asssociation
Rocky Mountain Brief Therapy Institute
Cochrane, Alberta, Canada

PREFACE

One of the things I love to do is help other people's ideas and words find their way into print and to provide practitioners with ideas from all sorts of places and angles that help them in their work, whether that is therapy, coaching, consulting, training, or what-have-you. The book you are holding helps fulfill that love. It is the culmination of many conversations, consultations, and e-mailings from people who love practicing in the solution-focused brief therapy tradition of Insoo Kim Berg and Steve de Shazer.

It has been several years since Insoo and Steve left us, but their presence is keenly felt in the work and trainings that continue. As I solicited submissions for this book, greater and greater ideas came forth: not only interventions and practices, but also stories, poems, think pieces, and, to my great delight, recounting of things that happened in therapy that could be considered "outrageous" and not very solution-like, but that nonetheless helped clients move toward their goals.

The book is organized loosely into sections on general practice, which includes working with specific populations and uses other than therapy; ideas for trainings; a miscellaneous section that includes stories, poems, and quotes useful for solution-focused thinking; a few pieces that are a bit theoretical in presentation; some very provocative pieces on "outrageous moments in therapy"; and a final section on resources that includes Steve de Shazer and Insoo Kim Berg quotes and an annotated bibliography of Steve's early books.

I hope that you find this book useful, thought provoking, and fun. I certainly have experienced all of those things while editing it.

Thorana S. Nelson

ACKNOWLEDGMENTS

Once upon a time (I won't mention how long ago), Terry Trepper encouraged me to edit a book that would provide the kinds of short, quick-read things that therapists and practitioners do that we tend to talk about over coffee or drinks at conferences, but seldom see in print. That was the birth of *101 Interventions in Family Therapy* (Nelson & Trepper, 1993). Since then, I have edited similar books with other coeditors (including John Frykman and Frank Thomas) and by myself (see references). Each one is special to me and has resulted in further interesting conversations over coffee and drinks at conferences and other places. None of them would have happened without the help and encouragement of my partners in crime: Terry Trepper, John Frykman, and Frank Thomas. May the banners of infamy ever wave!

I also would like to acknowledge the help of the editors at Routledge, including Marta Moldvai. Thank you to all the people in front of and behind the scenes in the book-publishing business at Routledge. My hat goes off to you.

My colleagues and friends in the Solution-Focused Brief Therapy Association (SFBTA) have been my inspiration and my reward for many years, leading and journeying with me in SFBT-land. It's been great and I look forward to many more years, experiences, and good times.

Finally, to four very special people: Steve de Shazer and Insoo Kim Berg, who were always intensely interested in how people were using their ideas and willing to talk about ideas and practices; Yvonne Dolan, who became my friend and colleague through special trainings with Steve and who has been my inspiration for seeing the best in every situation and in every person; and, without a doubt, Vic Nelson, my husband and best friend, who embodies a solution-focused life with wisdom, grace, and good humor. It doesn't get much better than this!

REFERENCES

Frykman, J., & Nelson, T. S. (2003). *Making the impossible difficult: Tools for getting unstuck.* Lincoln, NE: IUniverse.

Nelson, T. S. (Ed.). (2005). *Education and training in solution-focused brief therapy.* New York: Haworth.

Nelson, T. S., & Thomas, F. N. (Eds.). (2007). *Handbook of solution-focused brief therapy: Clinical applications.* New York: Haworth.

Nelson, T. S., & Trepper, T. S. (1993). *101 Interventions in family therapy.* New York: Haworth.

Nelson, T. S., & Trepper, T. S. (1998). *101 More interventions in family therapy.* New York: Haworth.

Thomas, F., & Nelson, T. (1998). *Tales from family therapy.* New York: Haworth.

THE EDITOR

Thorana S. Nelson, PhD, is a professor of marriage and family therapy in the Department of Family, Consumer, and Human Development at Utah State University, where she teaches theory, ethics, and research courses in marriage and family therapy, and supervises practica. Dr. Nelson graduated with a BS in psychology from the University of Houston and an MA and a PhD in counselor education with an emphasis in marriage and family therapy from the University of Iowa. She also teaches solution-focused brief therapy and other workshops for those who are interested. She has published numerous articles, book chapters, and books in the areas of family therapy and solution-focused brief therapy. She and her husband, Victor, live in Mendon, Utah, and have two children, two grandchildren, and two cats.

THE CONTRIBUTORS

Paul Avard
Coventry Education Department
Coventry, UK

Liselotte Baeijaert
Coach, consultant, trainer
1701 Itterbeek, Belgium

Kevin Ball
Psychoanalytic psychotherapist
    and family therapist
London, UK

Rob Black
Private practice
Bath, UK

Vicky Bliss
Brief Therapy Support Services,
    Ltd
Lancashire, UK

Gwenda Schlundt Bodien
The Agency for Solution-Focused
    Work
IJsselsten, Utrecht,
    The Netherlands

Tommie V. Boyd
Department of Family Therapy
School of Humanities and Social
    Sciences
Nova Southeastern University
Fort Lauderdale, Florida

Janet Campbell
Private practice
Bloomingburg, New York

Jeff Chang
The Family Psychology Centre
Calgary, Alberta, Canada

Heather Fiske
Private practice
Toronto, Ontario, Canada

Steve Freeman
United Kingdom Association for
Solution-Focused Practice
Ipswich, UK

Adam S. Froerer
Department of Clinical
Psychology
Argosy University
Chicago, Illinois

Evan George
BRIEF
London, UK

Bruce Gorden
Private practice
San Diego, California

Paul Hackett
Family therapist, private practice
Hackney, UK

Paul Hanton
Paul Hanton Consultancy Services
Yorkshire, UK

Arnould Huibers
Solutions Centre
Utrecht, The Netherlands

Chris Iveson
BRIEF
London, UK

Ian Johnsen
Brief Therapy Institute of Sydney
Sydney, Australia

Harriet E. Kiviat
Private practice
Boynton Beach, Florida

Harry Korman
Child and adolescent psychiatrist,
family therapist in private
practice
Malmö, Sweden

Mark Mitchell
Staff development and training
coach
Playa del Ray, California

Thorana S. Nelson
Department of Family,
Consumer, and Human
Development
Utah State University
Logan, Utah

Clare Scott
Integrated Services Program
The Mental Health Center
Boulder, Longmont, and
Lafayette, Colorado

Kathryn C. Shafer
Limitless Potentials
Jupiter, Florida

Lee Shilts
Capella University
Minneapolis, Minnesota
Private practice
Plantation, Florida

Dvorah Simon
Veterans Health Administration
Albuquerque, New Mexico

Joel Simon
Center for Solution-Focused
Practice
Walden, New York

Sara A. Smock
Marriage and Family Therapy
    Program
Texas Tech University
Lubbock, Texas

Anton Stellamans
Ilfaro
Bruges, Belgium

Tomasz Switek
Solutions Focused Approach
    Center
Warsaw and Inowroclaw, Poland

Lyndsey Taylor
Woodhouse Enhanced Primary
    Care Center
West Yorkshire, UK

Paolo Terni
Brief Coaching Solutions
Milan, Italy; Walnut Creek,
    California

Frank Thomas
College of Education
Texas Christian University
Fort Worth, Texas

Jay Trenhaile
Counseling and Human Resource
    Development
South Dakota State University
Brookings, South Dakota

Coert Visser
Coach, trainer
Driebergen, The Netherlands

Lorenn Walker
University of Hawaii Honolulu
    Community College
Honolulu, Hawaii

Carole Waskett
Northwest Solutions
Manchester, UK

Yulia Watters
PhD Candidate
Nova Southeastern University
Fort Lauderdale, Florida

John Wheeler
Trainer, supervisor, consultant,
    private practice
Gateshead, UK

Sue Young
General Teaching Council for
    England
East Yorkshire, UK

Brenda Zalter
The Credit Valley Hospital
Toronto, Ontario, Canada

Phillip Ziegler
Coach, consultant, trainer
San Francisco, California

I

Interventions and Practices

1

THE OPTIMAL ZONE SCALE

Coert Visser

The scaling question is the most popular question that emerged out of the solution-focused approach. This chapter describes step-by-step how you can use the scaling question. Here is an example. Some time ago, when I was talking with a client, an interesting variation of the scaling question emerged between the two of us, which I call the "optimal zone scale."

The woman I was coaching wanted to learn to be more assertive so that she could defend her personal boundaries and speak her mind on issues that mattered to her. This would help her to feel better at work and to keep her work load within acceptable limits. It would also help her colleagues. By being more assertive, she would be clearer to her colleagues, who would know then exactly what they could and could not expect from her. Also, she had noticed that colleagues tended to respect and value her more when she acted more assertively.

However, my client was also aware that she shouldn't go too far in speaking her mind. She realized that if she would take this too far she could become a shrew. She absolutely did not want that. She did not want her colleagues to become afraid of her or feel intimidated. Being friendly and helpful was one of the most important aspects of her work role. So she could not afford to lose those aspects of her behavior. When she was explaining this to me I drew the picture of the scale (see Figure 1.1). The picture visualizes that there is a zone in which her behavior is effective—the optimal zone—and two zones in which it isn't. On the left, she would be too little assertive; on the right she would be overassertive. This said, this visualization was very useful to her. She realized she was now slowly moving to the middle of the optimal zone.

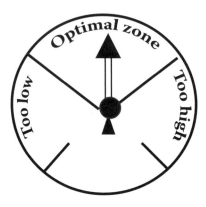

Figure 1.1 The optimal zone scale.

2

7-ELEVEN

Frank Thomas

INSTEAD OF THE MIRACLE QUESTION

"Let's say 6 months have passed after you finish therapy with me. We happen to run into each other at the local 7-Eleven. (Of course, I don't walk up to you—you walk up to me, in keeping with our confidentiality agreement.) You begin to tell me how the changes you experienced during our time together have continued. What do you tell me?"

I've found people put themselves into a present-tense conversation quite quickly; tell me what changed; and tell me what carried over/rippled. I like it a lot—less fantasy than the miracle question, in my opinion.

3

THE SOLUTION FOCUS
A Universal Tool

Carole Waskett

Many years ago I used to live on a boat. I was married to a boat builder who restored old wooden boats. There was often no electricity in the places where Roger worked, so he had a wondrous bag of old-fashioned tools. Amongst them was a hand drill, complete with a set of augurs and other drill bits. Some of the augurs were huge like rolling pins, while some of the other drills were delicate as needles. The drill's "mouth," as it were, was designed to grip the end of each of the various "bits," which Roger kept carefully wrapped in oiled leather. He and his drill were very comfortable together. It had a round wooden pad—I remember its crazed, worn surface, against which he would put pressure, to make the right-sized hole for the job in hand. He selected his bit carefully. He was so skilled that he hardly used any energy in drilling a hole. He knew just how hard to lean on the pad, holding the drill at the right angle, and turning the handle at exactly the right speed so that the resulting hole was perfect for its purpose. It was easy.

I think of the solution-focused approach (SFA) like that. With the right bit and a comfortable, experienced practitioner, it does the job sweetly and without fuss or pretension. Using the SFA, either as an assistant to someone else or as the protagonist ourselves, we use the same "handle"; we look for what's wanted (the platform, the goal). Then we wonder what the person/group knows already: What strengths, resources, past experiences will help them to move forward? Next we look at where they are now and how they got here (scaling) or, if appropriate, we might start helping the other person/group to construct their preferred future, and then follow up with scaling.

Finally, we look at the next small concrete step. Or, rather, we elicit it; it grows, almost organically, from the preceding conversation. It needs to be articulated clearly. It may be a very small step indeed, even a recognised, quiet movement or shift somewhere in the world of the process. The bit, once it bites, winds in tiny increments into the wood, and when it begins, it is virtually inevitable that forward movement will continue.

All through, we are curious, respectful, and relaxed. We don't try to do the tool's job for it; we just enable it to make the most of its own superb design.

So what kinds of bits are available? We can use the approach in a wide variety of ways: Obviously, for therapy; that's where the SFA began. Supervision follows the same path with appropriate boundaries and ethical responsibilities that maintain safety and clarity. In organisational work, we can discover where managers or teams want to go by asking questions that begin to bore into what is really wanted, and then staying behind the team (putting only gentle and appropriate pressure and encouragement on the pad) while they work out how to progress.

When we teach, we can discover and amplify the participants' strengths and already existing knowledge of the topic; we can always provide respectful opportunities for people to express what they know and how they are thinking. As well, we can make it a habit to ask what difference the teaching session will make if it "works," and what "work" means for this particular group. Scaling, too, is invaluable in any teaching session. Teaching is a mysterious business and needs plenty of respect, space, and air to allow learners to benefit.

These are only a few of the "bits"—the uses of the universal handle. In any situation where a preferred future and forward movement are relevant, solution-focused thinking seems to fit. I used it for myself in a tricky house move, making small steady steps in a worrying maelstrom of uncertainty, solicitors' letters, and the movements of what to me were large sums of money. "In good order, in good heart, and moving forward," I said to myself almost daily; the mantra was my goal at every stage, and it worked.

The wonder of the solution-focused approach is that it is strong, flexible, and reliable. Going back to the original metaphor, we need to buy a quality drill (ensure we're well trained and educated in the model); test, experiment, and practice a lot to become quiet and comfortable with it; and select the right bit. Some practitioners develop real expertise with a particular "bit." There are excellent therapists, for instance, who would baulk at consulting to help a team move forward in its work. Experience and success in the youth justice system may not predispose a practitioner to teaching adults.

On the other hand, some very experienced workers are confident and unfussed about working in any arena where the approach would be useful. This is often because the underlying element of the solution-focused approach—that of a respectful curiosity and the knowledge that people have the ability to progress—is in the forefront of their minds and practice. Any bit can be selected; the combination of a good reliable tool and a confident worker will get the job done.

4

SCALING AGENCY WITH CLIENTS WHEN THEY BEGIN TAKING ANTIDEPRESSANTS

Frank Thomas

A significant percentage of clients in the United States and other hard-currency countries take psychotropic medication for depression, anxiety, and other conditions. The research regarding the treatment of depression is quite clear: Those who receive both antidepressant medications and psychotherapy report greater change than those who receive only one or the other. When clients start taking antidepressants, the prescribing physician usually[1] tells them about the possible negative side effects, the expected positive effects from taking the medication, and the timetable within which most patients will experience both.

One of the most common things I hear clients voice is hope that the medication will alleviate their depressive symptoms. I agree with them—who would *not* want clients' problematic experiences changed for the better? However, I also take this conversation to be an opportunity to scale the person's agency, his or her ability to choose, in order to clarify my part in the change process and the clients' ideas about influence or control. I got this idea from Jonathan Prosser (1999, 2003), a UK psychiatrist who contributed to threads about medications and SFT on the SFT-L listserv, and from Steve de Shazer (1999), who proposed this idea on the topic of SFT and medications on the SFT-l listserv: "Luc Isebaert's question might be useful: 'So, how are you going to make this medication work for you? What are you going to do to help it work?'"

THE INTERVENTION

The intervention would follow a process much like this:

Week 1

Client: Oh, I wanted to let you know that I started taking _____ (anti-depressant) last week. I've been talking with my doctor. She agrees that I'm depressed, and she says this drug will help me feel better.

Therapist: OK, so you followed through with your doctor. How did you come to make that decision with her?

Client: [describes reasons for seeing the physician and process of arriving at the decision to try antidepressants]

Therapist: What did your physician say about what you could expect?

Client: [usually describes effects, negative side effects, and timetable for both]

Therapist: So…your doctor says you should feel the positive effects in 3 to 4 weeks, huh?

Client: Yes.

Therapist: And there may be negative side effects prior to seeing positive results?

Client: Yes.

Therapist: How do you see yourself coping with the negatives before you get the positives?

Follow-up questions: How else? How have you coped with negative effects outside your control in the past? What keeps your hope for change alive while you wait for the medicine to take effect?

Three weeks later

Therapist: So now that it's been several weeks since you started taking the antidepressants, have you noticed differences?

Client: [usually discusses negative side effects and the beginning of positive effects]

Therapist: What has helped you cope with those negative effects?

Client: [usually discusses his own resources and exceptions under his control]

Therapist: OK, so you say you have coped pretty well with the negative and are finally getting some positive effects. Yet at the same time, we've been meeting each week for counselling and you have reported these positive changes and exceptions:

(*list here, with details*). Many people experience even greater change in their depression (*client's word*) when they do "talk therapy" as well as medications. If you're like most people, I'm wondering: How much of your positive change do you attribute to the medicine, and how much of the changes in your depression seem to respond to making changes yourself? Put it into a percentage for me, if you can—it's just a starting point.

Client: [Invariably, the client assigns at least a small percentage to his own efforts toward change in therapy and in his daily living.]

Therapist: So, let's just focus on that part of you and your experience that you have some control over—that part of the changes you say is not the medicine. What's our next step regarding your depression, *just* in that area?

Follow-up questions: How do you see that as being under your control? How have you influenced that, on purpose? What does that say about your ability to influence part of your depression?

A Case Example

Jake and Eleanor contacted me for marriage counselling recently. Jake had suffered a heart attack 8 weeks prior to our first session, and they related that a lot of the stress that "caused"[2] his heart attack came from their unhappy marriage. Unbeknownst to me, Jake had an appointment with his cardiologist between the second and third marital therapy sessions and began taking an antidepressant. When he told me, I inquired about his decision, and he informed me that he had already been experiencing the negative side effects:

Jake: You know,....[rolls his eyes toward Eleanor]

FNT: Eleanor—what's he talking about?

Eleanor: You *know*...sex! [both giggle]

FNT: How is it that you can both giggle about this change?

Jake: Well, now that I can't...you know...we kiss a lot on the couch, and our 12-year-old son yells, "Ewwww! Gross!" [both laugh]

FNT: OK, how did you turn this negative side effect into something you can laugh about?

Jake: Well, we're both committed to getting through this, and I'm just so damn *hopeful* for the first time in years! *That's* the medication!

FNT: OK, so what part of the positive changes you've seen so far are directly related to the medication, do you think?

Jake: [relates his elevation in mood, increased hopefulness, cessation of suicidal thoughts, and other significant changes]

FNT: I couldn't be happier for you! You didn't mention other positive changes that you [looking at Jake] and the two [looking at Eleanor] of you tell me you've experienced lately. So let's put a percentage on it, just a "guesstimate":

What percentage of the positive changes you've seen in your marriage would you say are related to things *besides* the medicine?

Eleanor: Oh, I know several [she lists three]. We were doing these even before Jake started taking the medicine.

Jake: The medicine makes it easier for me to be positive, but I'm still the one who has to act on things. [Jake describes part of his miracle morning: snuggling, inviting everyone to cook breakfast with him, listening to his son without any criticism, and other aspects of his miracle.]

FNT: If it's OK with you, let's spend our time talking about the things you have a "say" in—we all seem to be in agreement that there are things you do in addition to the effects of the medicine that are having some great results....

Follow-up questions: How did you come to notice these positive changes? How do you keep them going? What else (*times five*)?

It is clear that Jake is benefiting from the medication; at the same time, he stated that he is committed to getting off the antidepressant medication "as soon as I think I can" because of the negative effects on their sex life. I plan to promote consultation with his physician throughout this process because stopping antidepressants (and many other medications, including alcohol) should only be attempted with medical supervision.

FINAL THOUGHTS

Therapists bring expertise to the counselling context, including general knowledge about medications. What one should never do is argue with a client about (a) seeking out medication (e.g., prescribing, unless one is licensed to do so), (b) the client's experience of the medication, or (c) stopping the medication. People attribute change to many sources—G*d, hard work, medications, circumstances, and luck, to name a few—and asking clients to assign percentages to agentive areas of their experience allows us to focus on that which they can influence. Gregory Bateson once said that we might have to divide up the world to make sense of it, but "no necessity determines how it shall be done" (1980, p. 42). Working on what works is our solution focus; determining what parts of experience clients see as being within their control is one way to work on what works.

NOTES

1. In the United States, there is a tendency for nonmedical psychotherapists to give their opinions regarding the medication type, dosage, and length of treatment patients receive. I am not a physician; therefore, I do not give medical advice. Consultation, with client permission, is the best clinical choice to take if one is to avoid "practicing medicine" without a medical license. I leave medical advice-giving with physicians.

2. It's interesting how many people attribute the causes of their heart attacks to stress, life decisions, and relationships. For more on this, see Crichton (1988) for a wonderful account from the acclaimed novelist's medical school training.

REFERENCES

Bateson, G. (1980). Every schoolboy knows... In *Mind and nature* (pp. 25–71). New York: Bantam.

Crichton, M. (1988). Heart attack! In *Travels* (pp. 60–66). New York: Ballantine.

de Shazer, S. (1999, July 27). SFT and ADHD. Downloaded August 18, 2008, from http://listserv.icors.org/

Prosser, J. (2003, November 19). Teaching docs. Downloaded August 18, 2008, from http://listserv.icors.org/

Prosser, J. (1999, July 26). SFT and ADHD. Downloaded August 18, 2008, from http://listserv.icors.org/

5

USING SCALING QUESTIONS TO ASSESS COUPLE READINESS FOR THERAPY

Lee Shilts

Scaling questions have been a favorite technique of mine for over 25 years. This powerful tool can be utilized in a variety of ways with a multitude of clients. In this chapter, I explain how I use scaling questions to assess couples' readiness for therapy.

SCALING QUESTIONS

Scaling questions expand both on exceptions and future visions. They invite clients to put their observations, impressions, and predictions on a scale from 0 to 10. For our discussion, it is important for the therapist to choose the appropriate scale from the unlimited possibilities based upon the relevancy to the clients. For example, solution-focused therapists make frequent use of confidence scales, determination scales, and effort scales. When working with couples, I have chosen two types of scales to use with my clients: motivation and optimism.

SCALING MOTIVATION AND OPTIMISM

It is useful for both the therapist and couple to know how motivated the couple is to work on building toward solutions. Couples' answers to a scaling question about how hard they are willing to work help in formulating end-of-session feedback. When working with couples, I ask the clients not only to scale their own level of motivation; I further ask each partner to predict the other's level of motivation toward positive change. Couples who indicate a high motivation to work are generally more likely to continue what has worked for them in the past and to try new strategies they suggest might be useful. The following example illustrates a couple who presented for therapy and scored high marks on motivation.

Therapist: Here is a different kind of question: On a scale of 0 to 10, I would like each of you to rate your personal level of motivation toward working for a solution regarding your relationship. You know, 0 would indicate that you currently have little motivation to work on the problem. On the other hand, a score of 10 would suggest optimal motivation to work on the problem. On the piece of paper I handed each of you, I want you also to predict what you think your partner will score as his or her level of motivation. Therefore, you will have two scores on your paper: One will be your own personal level of motivation. The second score will be the score you predict your spouse will record. Go ahead and record your scale scores. When you are ready, we will start with Peter's two scores.

Peter: Well, I know I want to save this marriage. So, my score for myself is quite easy. I put myself at a solid 10 regarding my level of motivation. I further believe Sophie wants the marriage to last. Therefore, I predicted her score quite high, and thought she would rate herself at about a 9.

Sophie: I too want this marriage to work. Therefore, I, too, rated my level at the optimum and gave myself also a 10. I was not that surprised that Peter gave himself a high score and I predicted his level of motivation to be at about an 8 or 9.

Therapist: These are very excellent scores and I too am not that shocked. From the beginning, I got the feeling that you two came into therapy willing to put forth some hard work to move toward workable solutions regarding your marriage. The scores do not lie. You both are extremely motivated to work toward change. What is even more revealing is that you each predicted that the other was motivated to save your marriage. Given these scores, I think we are ready to move forward.

This example is quite straightforward. However, not all couples come to therapy highly motivated to put in the hard work necessary to reach their goals. I have seen a wide variance of scores from partners and their predictions of their spouses. Two examples illustrate how I set the next stage for therapy.

Case Example: Bob and Dorothy

Therapist: Bob and Dorothy, I have a question I would like the two of you to think about and give me an answer. On a scale of 0 to 10, how optimistic are the two of you that you can move your current marriage situation to a better place? You know, 0 would indicate that you currently have no optimism that the marriage can work out. On the other hand, a score of 10 would suggest to me that you are supremely optimistic that you two can work together to solve your problems. On the piece of paper I gave to you, I want you also to predict how you think your spouse will score his or her level of optimism. Thus, you each will have two scores to report. One will be your own personal level of optimism. The other score will be where you think your partner currently is in his or her level of optimism. When you have your two scores, we will let Dorothy start first.

Dorothy: In regards to my level of optimism, I gave myself a very high mark. I rated myself at a 9 in regards to my optimism. I also predicted that Bob would rate himself quite high when it came to optimism, and I predicted he rated himself at an 8.5. Therefore, I see myself and Bob both highly optimistic that we can resolve our relationship differences.

Bob: I did not come up with exactly the same scores as Dorothy. Although I agree with her level of optimism and did predict that she would score herself quite high, I did not at the same time agree with how she predicted my own personal level of optimism. I predicted that Dorothy would rate herself in the 8 to 9 range. However, I rated myself at a 4 when it comes to how optimistic I am about resolving our issues.

Discussion. In this particular case example, we see partners who differ quite sharply with regard to their own personal levels of optimism for finding successful solutions to their marital problems. They both saw Dorothy as quite optimistic in resolving their issues. However, although Dorothy predicted that Bob would be high also with a score of 8.5, the reality was that Bob saw himself rather low in optimism and gave himself a score of 4. This is a rather large discrepancy in the partners' levels of optimism. As their therapist, I would need to deal initially with this discrepancy and increase Bob's optimism before moving forward in the therapeutic process.

DESCRIPTION OF INTERVENTION

Each partner arrives at a total of four different scale scores: motivation for self and partner, and optimism for self and partner. In all, there will be a grand total of eight scores for the therapist to analyze and discuss with the couple. Noting discrepancies will help the therapist and clients to derive a plan for moving forward with the therapy.

Case Example: Dick and Karen

Dick and Karen presented for therapy with me due to marital conflict. Dick had recently lost his job and with money problems and the stress of keeping their family going, the two came to therapy with little hope that they could keep their marriage afloat. What made their situation quite interesting was that both presented highly motivated to work on the marriage and both further predicted that the other was highly motivated to save the marriage. However, they each scored themselves low on optimism and subsequently predicted low optimism scores for each other. The following excerpt from the case illustrates the predicament for Dick and Karen.

Therapist: OK, you each have scored where you see yourself on the two scales, and you each further predicted the other's score on the same two scales. So, you each have four separate scores, two for optimism and two for motivation. Who would like to start?

Dick: I can go first. There is no doubt that I am highly motivated to save our marriage. I love Karen and despite our arguments want to remain married. So, I did not hesitate to rate myself at a 10 for motivation and I further predicted that Karen would be at a 9 or 9.5 in the area of motivation to work on our relationship. However, I cannot say that I feel so high in the area of optimism. I also think that Karen shares my same sense of low optimism. Therefore, I would score us both in the 3 to 4 range in regards to how optimistic we are that we can improve our relationship. This is just how honest I feel at the present.

Karen: How uncanny!! As Dick was explaining where he is at in all of this, I could not help but look at the scores I wrote down. They are almost a carbon copy of what Dick just presented. I, too, am highly motivated to work on the marriage and I have always thought that Dick also was motivated. That is the reason I think we are here tonight. I too gave myself a score of 10 and predicted that Dick would also score himself at a 10. So, in that area, we have no problem. However, I too have very little optimism that we can make it through all these difficult times. The stress around this marriage is often just unbearable. Thus, I gave myself a 3 in optimism and predicted Dick at a 2 to 2.5 at best.

Therapist: You two really know each other well and the numbers speak volumes as to where you guys are presently at. First, it is very encouraging that in spite of all the difficulties, you two are still highly motivated to save the marriage. You also sense this in the other person. It makes so much sense, Dick, when you say you still love Karen. I suspect you feel the same toward Dick, Karen. Second, given what you two have been through, it also makes sense that your levels of optimism are low. Therefore, I would like the two of you to do a couple of things for me between now and our next session. Continue to note your high levels of motivation and be prepared to tell me what keeps you motivated. Also, note things you see that would tell you that the other continues to be motivated. I would also like you each to note times this week when your levels of optimism are higher than what you currently report. What is going on when you feel more optimistic about the future regarding your marriage? I think you folks are off to a great start and I will see you in 2 weeks.

Discussion. In this particular case, I wanted to compliment the couple for their high degree of motivation to save their marriage. I further normalized their low optimism given their current life situation. Future sessions would focus on helping the couple maintain their motivation as well as to note times when they felt more optimistic in their relationship. In general, I would feel quite confident with this couple, given their scaling scores.

CLOSING COMMENTS

Scales allow therapists and clients to define a term (e.g., motivation) and a construct (a scale where 10 stands for the goal and zero stands for absence of such goal) simultaneously. They serve to represent multiple meanings as well as preserve much flexibility for change. Therefore, their utility in therapy is unlimited. This chapter hopefully demonstrates just one way a therapist can use scales to help couples assess their relationship and at the same time decide what they need to do to move their relationship to a better place.

6

SOLUTION-FOCUSED ASSESSMENT

Clare Scott

	Never				Always
I get enough rest and sleep.	1	2	3	4	5
I have people who understand me.	1	2	3	4	5
I have satisfying relationships.	1	2	3	4	5
I am able to calm myself when needed.	1	2	3	4	5
I have positive ways of coping with angry feelings.	1	2	3	4	5
I am satisfied with my home environment.	1	2	3	4	5
I am able to maintain my concentration and attention on activities that are important to me.	1	2	3	4	5

In the past week, on average, I have had	No drinks	1 to 3 drinks	4 to 7 drinks	8 to 14 drinks
In the last month, I have had five or more drinks on one occasion	Yes	No		

Notes:

7

A CONVERGENT COUPLE SCALE

Paul Hackett and Kevin Ball

INTRODUCTION

This idea grew in practice. I (PH) was behind the screen when Kevin came to consult the team. We were all wondering how to move forward with the couple Kevin was working with. I suggested using a couple scale; I even suggested this was something I had done before, although actually I hadn't. I guess that I sensed that Kevin was someone who would be prepared to take a risk in doing something different even if it was poorly described. After I watched Kevin's wonderful way of gently using this idea, I then utilised it with a couple I was working with who appeared equally stuck. In this chapter, we will describe the couple scale, offer two case examples, and consider pointers for further practice.

DESCRIPTION

Most people are aware of the usefulness of scaling questions and the questions that often flow from and through the scale, but often the scale can be quite sedentary: the therapist in her or his chair, asking the questions, although often the therapist's hands move as she or he asks the scale. In thinking about this, we thought that it might be enjoyable, educational, and different to get people to walk the scale. Often in our practice and in the practice of others, particularly with children, the corners of a room stand for the zero to ten of the scale (Hackett & Shennan, 2007). What we believe might be different here is in placing the couple at corners of the room, noting that the midpoint is what they are aiming for, and asking them to move to where they are now. This scale is useful when couples want to be closer or want some form of reconnection. In using this scale, we have to be clear that there is a shared goal: If one person is ambivalent about a relationship and another wants it to get better, it is unlikely that the scale will fit.

Thus, we describe to the couple that where they are standing at the corner of the room is the farthest they have felt from each other in relation to their goal and the midpoint is where they will feel they have achieved their goal. We ask the couple to move or not move to where they think they are now. The point they move to is from where we view the usual questions around the scale to flow. One difference we have noticed, though, is that the couple often answer the questions to each other rather than the therapist as they stand looking at each other rather than looking at the therapist. We have found that this often inculcates a sense of further closeness and intimacy.

In sharing our scale with others, people have commented that it is like enactment (Minuchin, Lee, & Simon, 1996), sculpting (Satir, 1983), or couples choreography (Papp, 1983). We are pleased to hear that it makes connections with a wonderful tradition of "doing something" in therapy and advise anyone interested to explore these wonderful ideas for fit in their own practices. Our intention in the first instance, though, was to do something different with the scale; any attendant benefits we view as a bonus. We hope that this rather abstract description will be clearer in our examples.

Example 1: Stepping Over Umbrellas

A couple Kevin saw had been struggling for a number of years with a multitude of difficulties, including mental health, financial, and relational. Kevin had a number of sessions with them before utilising the couple scale. It felt like they had to feel that they could trust him and that he understood their difficulties before they would consider a challenge to the sitting and talking.

Kevin asked the couple to move to corners of the room and explained how that was the furthest they were away from each other. He explained that the midpoint was what they were aiming for as a couple. The husband, ever a practical man, asked Kevin where midpoint was because he thought it helpful to know where he could walk to. We viewed this as wonderfully benevolent thinking because he did not want to walk on his partner's half of the scale. Luckily, the husband had brought an umbrella with him, and Kevin borrowed it and laid it down as the midpoint. This increased the sense of fun around this scale, but it also took the husband's wishes seriously and thus increased cooperation.

The couple moved to within about 2 feet each of the umbrella and Kevin asked them questions about why they were where they were. When asked how they would know when they had reached the umbrella point, the husband said that one of them would likely cross the umbrella. Kevin asked the husband to show him what it would be like if he crossed the umbrella. The husband crossed the umbrella and embraced his wife.

"When we get to this point," he said, "there will be more of this." Kevin suggested that they embrace (in private) for as long as they would like to whilst he took a break to talk to the team.

Example 2: Probing Deep Enough

A couple Paul saw had been struggling with numerous difficulties in their relationship that had been exacerbated recently by their children leaving home for university. They had previously seen a couple counsellor, but had been dissatisfied because they did not feel that the counselling "probed deep enough." They agreed that they wanted to stay together and make things work, but felt distant from each other. To avoid the trap of the same sitting and talking that may have characterised the previous counselling, Paul asked them to stand in opposite corners of the room and to imagine that this was the furthest distance they had felt apart from each other.

The female partner commented in a slightly joking way that it would be "further than this," so Paul took the opportunity to join in this sense of serious play and commented that the space between them might be measured in metres or miles, depending on the scale of the scale. Paul asked the couple to move to where they were that day in terms of closeness and the couple moved to within a yard of each other. Paul asked the couple what explanation they thought the other would give for why they had moved this distance and then suggested they take the smallest of small steps forward, perhaps barely perceptible.

In conversation afterward, Paul described how, as this was the first session, he did not want to try to make things too neat and that he thought the couple, as well as being vigilant for lack of challenge, would be vigilant in regards to suggestions that their difficulties could be easily solved. Paul then asked questions around what would be happening differently between them when they had made that smallest of small steps, who else might notice this, what else it might alter, and, of course, "What else?"

This was not the last session with the couple, but the scale was utilised in each subsequent session. The couple also reported that they had used the scale at home as a way of defusing tension between them.

POINTERS FOR FURTHER PRACTICE

Often our excitement for new ideas can obscure a necessary focus on the fit they have for our clients. Paul, like a lot of people, is the world's best therapist when he is behind the screen! In practice, he often discards ideas, knowing from experience that he has fallen for the idea outside of what might fit with his clients. So we offer a small note of caution: Ideas are only as good as the fit they have for clients—no more, no less.

In thinking about the couple scale, we discussed how, when working with a family, you could have people walking in from different points to converge on their shared goal. Guy Shennan from the Brief Therapy Practice in London suggested larger groups forming a circle, the edge of which is the zero of the scale, as a wonderful variation to our idea.

In essence we believe that the introduction of a sense of playfulness, of movement, and of difference through the use of converging scales encapsulates what we believe a solution-focused approach brings to helping clients. We invite you to try our scales where they fit and to let us know how it works out!

REFERENCES

Hackett, P., & Shennan, G. (2007). Solution-focused work with children and young people. In T. S. Nelson & F. N. Thomas (Eds.), *Handbook of solution-focused brief therapy: Clinical applications* (pp. 191–212). New York: Haworth.

Minuchin, S., Lee, W., & Simon, G. M. (1996). *Mastering family therapy: Journeys of growth and transformation.* New York: John Wiley & Sons.

Papp, P. (1983). *The process of change.* New York: Guilford.

Satir, V. (1983). *Conjoint family therapy* (3rd ed.). Palo Alto, CA: Science & Behavior Books.

8

"DIS-EASE" FREE
First Session Exercise

Kathryn C. Shafer

This exercise can be used with individuals, families, and groups of all ages.

BACKGROUND

In order to begin the therapeutic relationship, what can be helpful is discovering the image clients have of what is going to happen in therapy and the therapy session (Shafer & Greenfield, 2000). Often, changes have already taken place for clients prior to the first session (Berg & Miller, 1992). Helping clients identify their intentions right at the first session can be the essential element in treatment planning, goal setting, and establishing trust.

INTRODUCTION

The first session is viewed as high-impact time and may be the only encounter you ever have with these people. Once you introduce yourself by stating your name and title (and, if you are agency based, whether you are a social worker, doctor, nurse, etc.), find out their names, ages, how they got referred to you, and what happened that made them call you now as opposed to last week, last month, etc. This provides information about what types of clients they are and their motivation for change.

Next, ask the clients if they have ever been to a health care professional (like you) before. This helps establish dialogue and rapport with you as a professional, an educator, and a collector of information. Sometimes, clients don't understand what health care professionals in your capacity do, and explaining can help demystify and clarify myths they have about your role with them and what you can and cannot do. This helps establish trust, emphasizes strict adherence to their privacy and confidentiality, and relieves anxiety.

If they have seen professionals like us in the past, we are curious about this. We ask the clients if they found this past professional or therapy helpful and useful. The focus at this point is to pay careful, detailed attention to what clients report as helpful, because our job is to do more of this. If they report that the experience was not helpful or useful, our job is to again pay attention to what they report as not helpful. We want to make sure we do not repeat a situation that is not helpful, and we emphasize this with the client. You might even tell clients this is why you are asking these questions—which again is working on establishing the therapeutic relationship and trust in you as the professional.

For clients who have never been to a health care professional in your capacity, tell the clients that people who seek out or are brought to the attention of health care professionals are there in your office because they are experiencing their lives as being out of balance. There is something that is bringing them to you at this time that is requiring attention.

In your opinion as the professional, you ask them to consider this. This usually means that one or a combination of the following might be out of balance. This might be something in the mind (emotional), the body (physical), and/or confusion about religion or their spiritual lives. Your focus as the professional at this point is to help them understand that, when one of these areas or a combination is out of balance, that is when we seek professional help. Using "we" keeps the seeking inclusive, that maybe even you have sought out such help. You might again ask them what is bringing them to you now as opposed to 2 weeks ago, 1 month ago, etc.

Next, we ask the clients to consider that this discomfort or "dis-ease" may be due to what is occurring in the mind (beliefs held creating emotional suffering), the body (there is a physical symptom creating distress), or spiritually (there is some question about religion or faith). You continue to discuss with the client that when the person does not know what to do to bring this discomfort or "dis-ease" into balance, it is at this point that people reach out to some authority or health care professional, someone like yourself, to discover how to put what seems to be out of order back in order or into balance.

While you are having this conversation, you hand the clients a clip board or a pad of paper and a pen. This arouses curiosity; they wonder what you are going to ask them to do. At this point, you ask them if they have any questions. If you are seeing a couple or family, or conducting a group, give everyone a pad and pen to complete the exercise. This prevents individuals from copying or changing their answers based on what someone else answers. Plain white paper and colored pens are preferred to open the door to the clients' creativity and imagination and to keep the experience fun and curious.

Your only request of them is that until the exercise is finished, you want them not to speak or ask questions. Tell them to keep breathing because they often are paying such close attention to your every word that they stop breathing. They will have an opportunity to ask questions when the exercise is finished, and you will tell them the purpose of this exercise after they have answered the question.

Having clients write down the answer accomplishes several tasks:

It makes the invisible visible. You want to see (literally) what is on their minds and what they want from therapy, establishing the therapeutic contract.
You will see whether they can follow instructions (competency).
It serves as a mini-mental-status exam because at the end you ask them to sign it and write down the date.

When the instructions for the assignment have been reviewed with the clients, ask them whether they are ready for you to ask the question. They will nod, again establishing the "yes" set. Tell the clients you are going to ask them one question and you would like them to write down one or three answers in response to the question you ask. That's right: one or three—not two. Tell them what you are interested in is the first thoughts that pop into their minds. To help them understand, tell them that their answer or answers can be in the form of a thought, word, or phrase and can be as silly or as serious as they like, that they should not limit the answer, just please write down the first things that occur.

Ask them if they have any questions before you begin. Tell them if they are not sure how to answer the question, to look up at you and give you a confused look and you will ask the question in another way. Demonstrate the confused look if you want to make it fun. Then ask whether they are ready, further establishing the yes set. Then you say, "There is something that made you come to this office today. What do you want?" If they try to talk at this point, simply put your finger over your mouth (SHHHHHHHHH!) and ask them to please write down their answer or answers and look up at you when they are done. If the clients look up at you and give you the confused look, simply say, "You came here today because you either want or need something." Then repeat, "What do you want?"

Your job as the therapist is to wait patiently. Sit still, do not distract, talk, or engage the clients until they look up at you, letting you know they are finished. When the client, family, or group are all looking up at you, ask how many questions they answered. If people report that they have written two, ask them to write one more. This also may give you some information about such clients, such as having trouble understanding or following directions, refusing to cooperate, challenging rules or directions, etc.

Then ask the clients to sign their names and put the date at the top of the paper. Congratulations. You have just created the treatment plan established and created by the client. Have the clients read to you what they wrote and tell them this is what you are going to focus on in their work with you: the contract. What makes this exercise quite helpful and useful is that you have just completed several tasks at once. As stated earlier, you now know what the client wants (treatment contract), you found out if your client can follow directions (cognitive abilities), if a mini-mental-status exam was done (whether the client is oriented to date, time, and place), and you know if your client can read and write. Also, because this was created by clients, it is individualized to the clients' wants and needs. Your job as the therapist is to pay attention to what the clients want or need and stay there!

Clients sometimes ask how long they have to come to therapy. What you can offer to them is, "When this [showing them what they wrote down] is accomplished." Or, if they wonder on their way to the therapy appointment, "Why am I coming here?" or "I am not sure why I am still making appointments," you can tell them therapy is finished when what they have written is accomplished, or perhaps what they want or need has changed.

What also may be helpful at the first session is to suggest that they attend therapy in your office for three sessions, and that this session is considered number one. Since you have aroused their curiosity about how long therapy will take, you can tell them that they will know if they are making progress by the third session, which is letting you, the professional, know about whether therapy is helpful and useful to them; you are holding yourself accountable to them. It also helps establish how you both are on the journey together and that, even if getting what was wanted was accomplished by some exception or difference the two of you encountered (de Shazer, 1991), ultimately, the client must be satisfied with the therapeutic encounter.

REFERENCES

Berg, I., & Miller, S. (1992). *Working with the problem drinker: A solution-focused approach.* New York: W. W. Norton.

de Shazer, S. (1991). *Putting difference to work.* New York: W. W. Norton.

Shafer, K., & Greenfield, F. (2000). *Asthma free in 21 days: The breakthrough mind–body healing program.* New York: HarperCollins.

9

A COLOURFUL SOLUTION-FOCUSED GAME

Tomasz Switek

This kind of solution-focused game may be one tool during a group-building process. In this indoor or outdoor game, we support people to act together as a team, get into safe physical contact with team members, and on that basis follow two directions of conversation. The first one is connected with specific, future-oriented questions and the second is focused on analyzing present experience. People in small groups follow instructions they receive in envelopes.

INTRODUCTION

This game should be played in groups of four (three if four is not possible). For each group, prepare balloons, one big envelope, three or four small or medium envelopes, memory cards such as post-it or other small coloured paper, printed general instructions, and printed instructions for all four colours (see following discussion). Put instructions for each colour into small or medium envelopes you mark with the corresponding colour. Into the big envelope, put general instructions, the four envelopes with instruction for each colour, and the memory cards. Balloons simply should be available for participants.

After dividing people into groups of four, give each group a big envelope and ask people to follow instructions. That's all! Have a good time while observing participants.

GENERAL INSTRUCTIONS

Your instruction set includes:

1. One page of general instructions.
2. Four envelopes with tasks for each of you.
3. Memory cards that you can use to write down compliments for each other during the game.

Step 1. Get into groups of four (three if four is not possible). As a group, please pick one of the balloons that are around you in the room. You need just one balloon per group. You may take a second one in case yours breaks.

Step 2. Within your group, please decide together who will be which one of the following colours: **blue, green, red,** and **orange.** Please attribute one colour to each person. If you're a team of three, use just three colours.

Step 3. Now please walk together 20 metres (about 22 yards) in a direction chosen by your team. On your way, all of you need to hold the balloon with your *heads* only. Hands, arms, and other parts of your body may be used for many purposes apart from touching and holding the balloon. Try to enjoy the experience, going gently and softly as a team.

Step 4. So how was your 20-metre walk? Was it fun? You can congratulate each other on your cooperation. What worked well? What and how can you improve? Exchange your impressions. Now it is time to open the envelope addressed to the person who is **blue.** Please follow the included instructions.

Step 5. Now please go together 10 metres (11 yards) in a direction chosen by your team. Your task is to go and hold the balloon with your *necks* only. Hands, arms, heads, and other parts of your body may be used for many purposes, except touching and holding the balloon. Try to go, as a team, gently, softly, and having fun.

Step 6. So how was the trip? Were you flexible enough? You can thank each other for the experience. What worked well? What and how can you improve? Exchange your impressions. Now it is time to open the envelope addressed to the person who is **green.** Please follow the included instructions.

Step 7. Now, please jump together 10 metres in a direction chosen by your team. Your task is to jump and hold the balloon with your *arms* only. Hands, heads, and other parts of your body may be used for many purposes, except touching and holding the balloon. Try to jump, as a team, gently, softly, and having fun.

Step 8. So how about the jumping? Was it more like rabbit style or kangaroo style? You can thank each other for the experience. What worked well? What and how can you improve? Exchange your impressions. Now it is time to open the envelope addressed to the person who is **red.** Please follow the included instructions.

Step 9. Now please run together 10 metres in a direction chosen by your team. Your task is to run and hold the balloon with your *bellies* only. Hands, heads, and other parts of your body may be used for many purposes, except touching and holding the balloon. Try to run, as a team, gently, softly, and with fun.

Step 10. Were you still able to breathe after the run? Is your breath deep and fast enough? You can thank each other for that experience. What worked well? What and how can you improve? Exchange your impressions.

Now it is time to open the envelope addressed to the person who is **orange.** Please follow the included instructions.

Step 11. Find a way to round off this short game as a team. Then do it and come back to the main group!

INSTRUCTIONS FOR THE BLUE ENVELOPE

Please think about the topic written below and talk about it with your team. You are invited to have a conversation, but you can also try to show or perform it in any way you want! If you had as much determination as Rocky Balboa, what would you do differently in any "life fights" in the nearest future?

Task for the other team members. Listen carefully and ask and/or summarize when needed. Try to co-create and be part of the conversation around the story told by the person with **blue.** At the end of the conversation, you can write compliments on the memory cards for the storyteller and give them to her/him.

INSTRUCTIONS FOR THE GREEN ENVELOPE

Please think about the topic written below and talk about it with your team. You are invited to have a conversation, but you can also try to show or perform it in any way you want! If you had as much "resource sensibility" and "crime sensibility" as Colombo did, what would you do in a different way in any "life investigations" in the near future?

Task for the other team members. Listen carefully and ask and/or summarize when needed. Try to co-create and be part of the conversation around the story told by the person with **green.** At the end of the conversation, you can write compliments on the memory cards for the storyteller and give them to her/him.

INSTRUCTIONS FOR THE RED ENVELOPE

Please think about the topic written below and talk about it with your team. You are invited to have a conversation, but you can also try to show or perform it in any way you want! If you had as much trust in others as hobbit Frodo did, what would you do differently in any life choices in the near future?

Task for the other team members. Listen carefully and ask and/or summarize when needed. Try to co-create and be part of the conversation around the story told by the person with **red.** At the end of the conversation, you can write compliments on the memory cards for the storyteller and give them to her/him.

INSTRUCTIONS FOR THE ORANGE ENVELOPE

Please think about the topic written below and talk about it with your team. You are invited to have a conversation, but you can also try to show or perform it in any way you want! If you had as much passion about something as Winnie-the-Pooh did about honey, what would you do in a different way in any "life cooking" situations in the nearest future?

Task for the other team members. Listen carefully and ask and/or summarize when needed. Try to co-create and be part of the conversation around the story told by the person with **orange.** At the end of the conversation, you can write compliments on the memory cards for the storyteller and give them to her/him.

I have tried to be brief in describing the concept of dominoes and its rules. You can get all instructions in a ready-to-print format or ask questions by writing to tomaszswitek@centrumpsr.eu

10

"VISITOR," "COMPLAINANT," "CUSTOMER" REVISITED

Phillip B. Ziegler

In the MRI brief therapy literature, the terms *visitor, complainant,* and *customer* frequently appear (e.g., Fisch, Weakland, & Segal, 1982; Watzlawick, Weakland, & Fisch, 1974); they have been adopted by solution-focused brief therapy (SFBT) as well (De Jong & Berg, 2007; de Shazer, 1985, 1988, 1991, 1993, 1994). These terms are intended to guide the brief therapist in determining what kinds of interventions might be most useful with a given client based on his or her current readiness to work toward specific goals in therapy. The developers and authors are quick to explain that these terms are meant to refer to *the relationship* and not *the client*. This distinction is stressed to guard against labeling the client, eschewed in these approaches, and to maintain a systems perspective, while, at the same time, providing a pragmatic way of assessing the client's current readiness to work actively in therapy.

I was, and continue to be, surprised by SFB therapists' use of these terms even with the proviso. Steve de Shazer and Insoo Kim Berg, the developers of SFBT, so clearly understood that words matter. Words like visitor, complainant, and customer are, by their nature, descriptive of individuals. A visitor is someone who is visiting, a complainant is a person who is complaining, and a customer is a ready buyer. Saying that these words refer to relationships and not to clients does not solve the problem. Once we begin to use these terms, it is hard not to view someone who has been mandated for therapy as a "visitor" or someone who comes in complaining about her spouse, her parents, or her boss, or wanting to talk at length about her problems as a "complainant." Correspondingly, we naturally tend to strap ourselves with the responsibility as experts, to turn these people into "customers."

For a time I found it more clinically useful, both in therapy and consultation, to use role-designating terms such as "visitor/host," "complainant/sympathizer," and "customer/consultant" as a way of emphasizing the bipersonal nature of the therapeutic relationship. This approach allowed me to assess in clinically useful ways what roles the client(s) and I were taking in our therapeutic relationship at any given point. In this way, I was able to determine whether we were matching or working at cross purposes. If it appeared to me that a client was taking a "visitor" role, I would initially engage with her by being a good host. If a client presented in a "complainant" role, wanting to tell me about the difficulties she was facing in life, I would take a sympathizer's role, doing my best to convey to her my understanding of her concerns, frustrations, complaints, and perspectives, and to respond empathically. In both these situations, while I would begin by matching my role to the client's, I would be looking for and taking opportunities to transform the relationship into a "customer/consultant" relationship.

Over the years, as my work became more and more solution oriented, I also became more collaborative in my approach. Now I view my work less as "therapy" and more as a kind of consulting or coaching. The therapeutic enterprise with each client is custom designed with and for that client. Throughout therapy, the process is continually revised based on the client's reports as to whether what we are doing together is making a difference or not. If it is, we do more of what we've been doing, and, if not, we do something different.

It is a fundamental principle in SFBT that the client is expert with respect to the goals of therapy. I came to see, however, that the client also had a great deal of expertise about how therapy should go, how we could best work together, and even what and how I could contribute most effectively. I have come now to believe that my real expertise as an agent of change is in knowing how to help each client uncover and utilize his or her own ideas, temperament, theories, and experiences in designing and executing his or her own therapy. Bohart and Tallman (1999) make a strong case for the proposition that clients, not therapists, are the true active agents of change; therapists are more like midwives than birth mothers.

As my clinical role and my views about therapy evolved, I began attending more and more to what I saw as shifting roles that clients and I would take during one or a series of conversations during a session. Rather than trying to name our respective relationship roles, I began asking myself, "What kind of *conversation* are we engaged in at this moment in time?" People are hard if not impossible to change. Relationships are almost as hard to change. Conversations, on the other hand, are relatively easy to change, especially if one is aware of the roles each participant is taking and is skillful at inviting changes in those roles.

What role am I taking? What role is the client taking? What role is the client inviting me to take right now? Do I want to accept his invitation or invite him into customer/consultant conversation? If I am going to decline the client's invitation in order to invite her into a different kind of conversation, how can I do that most skillfully and respectfully? What question might I ask as a way to offer that invitation? What should I do if he declines my invitation and reinvites me into a visitor/host or complainant/sympathizer conversation?

My expertise, I've come to believe, is in being skilled in the art of influencing clients toward engaging in customer/consultant conversations and then in knowing how to participate in these conversations in therapeutically furthering ways. Insoo Kim Berg called this "leading from behind" (Cantwell & Holmes, 1994) or "a tap on the shoulder" (Berg & de Shazer, n.d.).

Being able to recognize what kind of conversation is occurring is extremely helpful; knowing also how to invite, respectfully decline, and offer counter-invitations are essential skills. But if we don't know what kind of conversation we are having with the client, we run the risk of participating endlessly in conversations that don't further the therapeutic enterprise and/or rebuffing the client in ways that lead to premature termination. I will finish this discussion by providing examples of the three types of conversations that take place in therapy: (a) visitor/host, (b) complainant/sympathizer, and (c) customer/consultant. The following examples come from our book on couple therapy (Ziegler & Hiller, 2001), so they emphasize conversations in couple therapy. But the principles apply as well to individual and family therapy.

VISITOR/HOST CONVERSATIONS

Mandated clients come to therapy because someone has ordered them to do so, often under some threat. Such clients begin conversations with us (assuming we can get them to talk at all) by telling us (a) there is no problem; (b) if there is a problem, it is someone else's problem; and/or (c) if there is a problem, they don't think therapy is the way to deal with it. For example, a man might come to a first session and explain that he doesn't believe in therapy and has come only because his wife is threatening to leave him if he refuses to seek professional help. He is inviting me to enter into a visitor/host or possibly a complainant/ sympathizer conversation. I want to respond initially by accepting his invitation. This means welcoming him and acknowledging and validating his experiences and feelings about the relationship and his feelings and attitudes about therapy.

If and when I sense that the client feels met on his own terms, I will, in turn, initiate some possible shifts in our conversation, tentatively inviting him into customer/consultant conversations, but not pressing it unless he seems to accept my invitation. I might, for example, ask a common solution-focused question with mandated clients such as, "Do you think it would be useful for us to work together to figure out what you might do that would get your wife to say you don't have to come here anymore?" This question invites him into the beginning of a customer/consultant conversation. If, by the end of the session, his views haven't changed, I thank him for coming and talking with me, and let him know that he is welcome to return in the future if at some point he thinks I might be helpful to him.

COMPLAINANT/SYMPATHIZER CONVERSATIONS

In couple therapy, the most common initial conversations that partners want to have with the therapist are complainant/sympathizer conversations. When people seek therapy for help in solving their problems, they frequently expect and need to spend some time talking about what is troubling them. Each partner wants to tell us how bad it is, how the other partner has been causing all the trouble, and why the other should change. These are all invitations into complainant/sympathizer conversations. It is imperative that we respond skillfully, respectfully, and sensitively to both partners, accepting both of their invitations by being good sympathizers while managing to convey to both partners that we are on both of their sides. (*Active neutrality* is a term Tobey Hiller and I borrowed from Harlene Anderson, 1997, and Anderson & Goolishian, 1992. We devote a chapter in our book to this issue in Ziegler & Hiller, 2001.)

When partners present with antagonistic, adversarial postures, it is counterproductive to make immediate efforts to point them out, shift the type of conversation, or decline the kind of dialogue the couple is initiating. A therapist who tries to force a particular conversational direction rather than maintain a posture of curiosity, compassion, and calm does so at his or her peril. But, as the partners come to feel understood, viewing the therapist as sympathetic to their plight, and sense that the therapist is not distressed in the face of intense conflict or expressions of strong negative feelings, opportunities almost always arise in which we can then invite each partner into customer/consultant conversations.

CUSTOMER/CONSULTANT CONVERSATIONS

Customer/consultant conversations rarely, but do occasionally, take place in the first few minutes of an initial therapy session. In most cases, they take some preparation and are usually initiated by me after accepting and participating in the kinds of conversations described earlier. However, my working assumption is that every client who enters my office is a potential customer in search of a consultant. The question is not whether he is motivated but rather, "What changes or goals might he be motivated to work for?" and "Am I a person who could help in that undertaking?" As we continue talking in visitor/host or complainant/sympathizer conversations, I listen and ask for opportunities to move our conversations in a direction that might facilitate this person's experiencing meaningful changes in his life. If our conversation produces even slightly positive answers to these musings, we are on the road to a positive outcome to our therapeutic enterprise.

REFERENCES

Anderson, H. (1997). *Conversation, language and possibilities: A postmodern approach to therapy.* New York: Basic Books.

Anderson, H., & Goolishian, H. (1992). The client is the expert: A not-knowing approach to therapy. In S. McNamee & K. Gergen (Eds.), *Therapy as social construction* (pp. 25–39). Newbury Park, CA: Sage.

Berg, I. K., & de Shazer, S. (n.d.) *A tap on the shoulder: 6 useful questions in building solutions* [CD]. Solution-Focused Brief Therapy Association (http://www.sfbta.org).

Bohart, A. C., & Tallman, K. (1999). *How clients make therapy work.* Washington, DC: American Psychological Association.

Cantwell, P., & Holmes, S. (1994). Social construction: A paradigm shift for systemic therapy and training. *Australian and New Zealand Journal of Family Therapy, 15*, 17–26.

De Jong, P., & Berg, I. K. (2007). *Interviewing for solutions* (3rd ed.). Monterey, CA: Brooks–Cole.

de Shazer, S. (1985). *Keys to solution in brief therapy.* New York: Norton.

de Shazer, S. (1988). *Clues: Investigating solutions in brief therapy.* New York: Norton.

de Shazer, S. (1991). *Putting difference to work.* New York: Norton.

de Shazer, S. (1993). Commentary: de Shazer and White: Vive la différence. In S. Gilligan & R. Price (Eds.), *Therapeutic conversations* (pp. 112–120). New York: Norton.

de Shazer, S. (1994). *Words were originally magic.* New York: Norton.

Fisch, R., Weakland, J., & Segal, L. (1982). *The tactics of change: Doing therapy briefly.* San Francisco: Jossey–Bass.

Watzlawick, P., Weakland, J., & Fisch, R. (1974). *Change: Principles of problem formation and problem resolution.* New York: Norton.

Ziegler, P. B., & Hiller, T. (2001). *Recreating partnership: A solution-oriented, collaborative approach to couples therapy.* New York: Norton.

11

APPRECIATING WHAT WORKS IN THE NATIONAL HEALTH SERVICE

Carole Waskett

I'm facilitating a summer "awayday" for a clinical team battling the weight of National Health Service (NHS) expectations. Optimum targets should be "stretching but not impossible," apparently. Those handed down from above for this team seem all but impossible, what with a couple of team members on maternity leave, a clinician's post still unfilled after someone left, and an ongoing debate about whether this busy team needs more than 6 hours a week of administration time. Oh, and that tiny, cramped office where everyone shares desks.

And yet, they have a short waiting list, a habit of taking care of each other, and a lot of laughter. Their team leader flies between them at lunch, which is a delicious feast of shared contributions, as there was no funding for food. She's checking on everyone, a joke here, a hand on the arm there, a pause to draw a quiet one into a conversation. It's obvious they like each other and care passionately about their jobs and their patients.

Later, they tell me that X, their senior manager, who rarely meets them as a team, has passed down the message: "Don't worry. I'll let you know if there's anything wrong." Their faces fall as they admit to wanting some praise and appreciation. "It wouldn't cost anything," somebody says longingly. The team leader, who meets with X regularly, does her best. "He does think we do well. I've heard him mention it to a couple of the other associate directors in the corridor," she says. Three people at once burst out, "But why doesn't he tell US?" And someone else adds, "And we invited him to come today; why isn't he here, at least for an hour?" It's a situation I come across too often, not just in our organisation but in others too.

My job, by the way, is a wonderful privilege. It entails supporting the staff in a variety of ways. I teach peer supervision, support staff teams and run team awaydays, and now and again do some individual coaching, 360-degree feedback, and similar things. I'm allowed to roam across the area, getting to know many of the great people here. I know that this organisation is stuffed full of talent, intelligence, and big hearts at all levels. And that sort of goodness needs nourishing with expressions of recognition and appreciation, not once a year, but often.

So how can we infiltrate appreciation into a culture that just isn't used to it? These are tough, battle-hardened British professionals who squirm at a compliment. Can solution-focused (SF) thinking help? I think so; it certainly helps me every day. Little steps are best. Here are some of the ways I'm experimenting with:

- Taking it gently: being curious about success rather than slathering on the praise: *"That seems so hard to do, and yet you seem to be turning it around and winning; how on earth…so what was the very first thing…how did you think of that?"*
- Using a compliments exercise in team events: *"Everyone please take a big piece of paper and write your name at the top. Now, everyone else is going to write something they appreciate about you—it may be a professional skill or perhaps something personal, like a great sense of humour. Please take your time and think carefully about each person. Off you go."*

I try to appreciate every little thing anyone says in an awayday, a teaching session, or a one-to-one conversation, treating each contribution like a gift from an honoured guest and being genuinely curious about any sign of stability (often highly prized in our storm-tossed NHS culture) or progress.

- Starting "positive rumours": *"Of course, you have a jewel of a secretary, don't you? Did you know she's just put herself through a counselling course outside working hours? That takes some commitment, I should think."*
  "Your receptionist is so impressive—I've just watched her with a patient, a deaf old man who seemed rather cross—she dealt with the situation so respectfully and effectively—and with a big restless queue watching as well."

- Hearing individual stories: I've noticed how the more senior managers (the ones the clinicians complain about) are working at full stretch for long hours with complete and extraordinary dedication and loyalty to those above them. On the whole, they want to support their staff, to be human and kind; many, after all, have come from the ranks of clinicians they now manage. But there is ferocious pressure from above—pressures of deadlines, mastering technical documents, attending demanding meetings, and, ultimately, dealing with the brutal forces of the highest levels of politics. There is no time for anything but the barest sinews of action. They toughen up, but there is still tenderness, empathy, and kindness there. When we have a chance to talk, I manage to clear my mind and listen with appreciation. And when I can, I ask, *"How do you manage to get through a day like you've just described? What keeps your heart up?"*

When I teach, SF thinking carries me through. Participants know more than they realise, and they can learn from each other. I do my best to model, suggest, and encourage mutual recognition and compliments. People are shy at first, and then take to it. Individuals move toward greater mutual encouragement and support, just like that wonderful team I first described. People do it already. When it's noticed and appreciated, they want to do it more. Notice those little diamonds of kindness—dig them out of the mud for a bit of spit and polish—recognise, articulate, amplify, do more—haven't we heard this somewhere before?

12

SPARKLING MOMENTS

Evan George

A colleague, Maggie Stephenson, asked me some time ago to join her to work with the senior management team of a high school for just one day, a day that she was going to follow up with a series of twilight meetings. The school had been in some difficulties and was working very hard to turn itself around. Amongst the many actions that they had already taken—new staff, refurbishment of much of the school, and new school uniforms, they had also requested this day's consultation to focus on the school, its future, and the best way to move forward as part of an ongoing project.

The morning was straightforward. The group worked on their "best hopes" for the process. They decided that they wanted the day to support them in becoming a school that "did full justice to the talents and abilities of the pupils and the talents and abilities of the staff." Maggie and I then asked them to define who the key stakeholders were in the life of the school and they developed a long list including staff, students, parents, local education authority and local community, residents who lived near the school, school inspectors, and many more. Much of the rest of the morning was spent with the members of the management team divided up into small groups, who were allocated a number of the key stakeholders each and asked to describe in detail what a "school that did justice to all the talents of staff and students" would look like. Sharing the work of the groups with the whole group built up a beautifully rich description of the school that they wanted to build.

However, by now we were just before the lunch break and it seemed to Maggie and to me that, in building this picture, the group had heightened the distance between where they were at present and where they wanted to be. We worried that lunch might be a rather downcast affair. So, on the spur of the moment, we asked the team to go back into their working groups and I found myself suggesting that in the minutes before lunch they might like to bring to mind those "sparkling moments[1] from school life that gave them hope that they could indeed become the school that they aspired to be." They did; they shared their stories and lunch was the better for it. The afternoon was structured around a set of scale exercises that built hopefulness and allowed them to begin to describe what just one point up the scale might look like, and what it might look like from the perspectives of all their key stakeholders. The day ended well and was judged by the participants to have been of use to them.

Some days later, I was meeting with a reconstituted family: a mother and her three daughters and a father and his son who had come together in tough circumstances. Family life was not easy and they had the idea that they might not be able to make it through together if things did not change.

I started the session by moving round the group, the four children and two adults, asking all of them for their "best hopes" from the session. As it happened, they each gave an answer that related to the idea of getting on better. Back round the group, asking each now to answer the question, "What difference will it make to family life if you find yourselves getting on better in the way that you want?" Each, including the 6-year-old, answered and elaborated a developing picture from each of their perspectives of a family life with fewer arguments, less conflict, and more getting on.

I then took a break in the session and asked them while I was out of the room to bring to mind "sparkling moments in family life that give you hope that you can indeed be the family that you aspire to be." On returning after about 5 minutes, I asked each of them in turn what they had recalled and each told a story, a "sparkling" story of family life that gave them hope. The stories differed: adult stories, teen stories, and child stories. As the father finished his account, he said, "We can do it, we can do it."

And that was the end of the session. It turned out to be both the first and last time that the family needed to come to BRIEF. As an intervention, this seemed to me to be amongst the most minimal that I could imagine: merely a description of what each family member hoped for from the therapy, how each would know that what he or she hoped for was happening, and then an anecdote from each—an account of something that had happened that gave hope that the family could change. The worker took no responsibility for defining the way forward, leaving that to the family members themselves.

NOTE

1. Borrowed from Freedman, J., & Combs, G. (1996). *Narrative therapy: The social construction of preferred realities.* New York: Norton.

13

A SINGING MIRACLE

Mark Mitchell

The singing question is simply an extension of the miracle question. It goes something like this: "And suppose the miracle happened or was starting to happen, and you started singing a song the next day. What song would you be singing that would tell you that the miracle was starting to happen?"

The question came as a result of a group session I had with some high school students during a critical incident debriefing session during the 1991 Los Angeles riots. I asked the miracle question of the group and a girl chimed in that she would know a miracle had happened if "we had gotten past this stuff [the rioting on campus] and were singing." So I followed up with, "And what would we be singing that would tell us the miracle was starting to happen?" She replied, "We would be singing 'We Shall Overcome.'" So I suggested to the group that we try singing the song. The group responded and sang. It was a very emotional moment in a dramatic situation.

Since then, I have experimented with the singing question in hopes of ensuring the start of the miracle. It is an attempt to find the "preferred feeling" that says the miracle is happening without depending on a verbal description. I have found that children and artists seem to respond to the question more positively than others. They seem to come up with songs more readily. Sometimes on school campuses, I run into children I have worked with and say to them, "Ooh…let me hear your song!" and they sing a little of it, reporting feeling better.

In thinking about this singing question, I started to realize that humans frequently turn to song and music to get through tough times. This is evident in churches, civic gatherings, and family gatherings. It has always been a way to change the biology and create a small miracle of feeling better.

14

A CLINICAL EXERCISE

Common Ground

Heather Fiske

I frequently ask clients to make lists of ways that they have "common ground" with a person in their lives with whom they also have important differences. I might give this as a "homework" suggestion. Most often, they will have mentioned some common ground in the conversation and I reflect that to them, write it in my notes at the time to reinforce it, and then begin the list with the title, "Common Ground," as part of giving feedback.

With couples, families, teams, or groups, the similarities and differences in their lists often generate further useful conversation. With individuals, the person may utilize the list to shift perspective, and sometimes I also ask him or her to imagine, or to ask, what the other person would say. The "common ground" phrasing seems to be especially useful, and I have been struck by how often clients begin to talk about "standing on," "retreating to," "rediscovering," "getting back to," "resting in," or even "spending the weekend at" their common ground.

15

USING SCALES WITH MULTIPLE GOALS

Coert Visser

Sometimes, people wonder about whether scaling questions are too simple to be used in complex real-life situations. In such situations, often there are multiple goals instead of only one goal, such as improving commercial skills. Moreover, often these goals are interrelated in one way or the other, or they may be competing with each other. An example may be the case of a company in which one group advocated the use of proactive environmental practices; they objected to the abundant use of plastic covers around certain products. Another group in this company insisted that the focus of the company should be achieving financial goals. The tension between these two groups grew to rather unpleasant proportions when members of both groups started accusing each other of all kinds of bad intentions and behaviors. A solution-focused coach was hired to solve this matter. To everyone's surprise, the parties were again on speaking terms within one session and fully cooperating within two brief sessions. What happened?

The first thing the coach did was to listen carefully to both parties, trying to understand their goals. After that, the coach suggested a framework in which the relationship between both goals was visualized.

Then, the coach asked them what they considered the most desired position in the matrix in Figure 15.1. They immediately agreed that C was the preferred place to be. The solution-focused coach drew a scale that looked like Figure 15.2. Next, he asked the group whether this scale represented their goals adequately, to which all of them agreed. Then

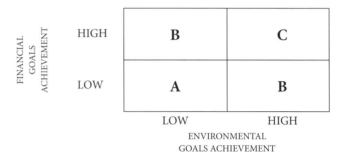

Figure 15.1 Financial and environmental goals.

he asked them to consider this scale and discuss with each other where they saw themselves now on this scale.

The coach then used all the familiar parts of the scaling questions. A bit to their own surprise, the group members started to agree more and more and discovered that there were some very interesting opportunities to improve both environmental and financial

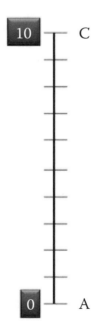

Figure 15.2 Goals scale.

performance at once. For instance, they indeed started to use fewer plastic covers, which was not only desirable from an environmental standpoint but also lowered direct costs and production time. One member called these "low hanging fruits." What is interesting is that, in the second session, the group became more united. The financial people showed increasing enthusiasm for the environmental goal and vice versa.

16

FOCUS ON MICROPROGRESSION IN SOLUTION-FOCUSED CONFLICT RESOLUTION

Gwenda Schlundt Bodien

Attending to microprogression is an important intervention in solution-focused conflict resolution. Microprogression is the progression toward achieving positive goals that participants show in a very small and subtle manner. By noticing microprogression and by acknowledging it, further progress is stimulated. Can you detect the microprogression in the following dialogue?

Peter and Lee are in conflict with each other and are having a session with a solution-focused coach to overcome their issues.

Peter: I have heard that Lee has said to another colleague of ours that I am not to be trusted! If that is his view, then what he actually says is that I am a liar. I am not having it! These sorts of accusations are what make him impossible to work with! This session is useless and doomed, because he just doesn't want things to improve. I won't stay if he doesn't apologize!

Coach (looking at Peter): Ah...so you have heard that Lee has said that you are not to be trusted. And since you really want this session to be useful for improvements between the two of you, you find it important to address this issue first?

Peter: Yes, of course I don't want to waste my time. If this issue is not resolved, this session is a complete waste of time. It can only be useful if Lee believes me when I say something! And I don't want him to say to other people that I am not trustworthy!

Lee stumbles and says a few words, ending his sentence like this: "I can't remember what I said…I know I was upset when I spoke with our other colleague."

Coach (looking at Peter): How would you notice that addressing this topic today has not been a waste of time…that it has been beneficial to further improvements between the two of you?

Peter (looking at Lee): Well, uh…if you are upset about something, why don't you come to me…tell me…don't gossip behind my back.

Lee: Yeah, well, when you hear something like that from another colleague…Why don't you come to me instead of starting a session like this one in such a negative way? As if this helps us any.…

Coach: So you both want this session to be worthwhile…leading to real improvements. That's why you both are prepared to address difficult topics. Openly and honestly. You both prefer it when your colleague just sits down with you for a chat to ask questions and discuss topics. Is that correct?

Peter: Yes, without honesty we'll never get where we want to be. I just want to be absolutely convinced you will address topics directly with me. Now he just talks to everybody but me.

Lee: Yeah…sure. But you have a tendency to get very angry very quickly. A week ago you said something I didn't understand, and when I started to ask you about it, you just got angry with me. That's what upset me…that's when I had to talk to my other colleague. I just don't understand why you got so angry.

Coach: You would like to understand what Peter meant when he said what he said last week…and you want to discuss this in an open and constructive way.…What would you like to ask him regarding this topic?

Did you detect the microprogression? The first example of microprogression is where Peter says he is prepared to leave. His reason for this threat to leave is because he wants this session to be useful. The second example of microprogression is where both Lee and Peter agree that honesty is important to them. They both have a yes-set regarding honesty and talking about issues with each other instead of with other colleagues.

Because the progression is so small, we call it microprogression. Noticing microprogression and using it has a positive impact. A good way to use microprogression is to summarize what has been said, using slightly more positive words. This is called reframing. Reframing means summarizing what has been said using just slightly more constructive words. These sorts of summaries have a mutualising effect. Mutualising means summarizing in such a way that all parties can agree with the summary. A solution-focused coach addresses a common interest or a common good intention to which all parties say yes. These interventions help to make small progress in a conflict. Microprogression is a subtle and small platform to success.

An example of a solution-focused intervention in a conflict resolution is the following. Suppose a solution-focused coach works with a team of eight people and one manager. The team members are in conflict with the team manager. The coach has been asked to talk to the team members first, then with the team manager, and then with the team members and the team manager together. A solution-focused intervention can be structured as follows:

SESSION WITH THE TEAM MEMBERS

The coach starts with the team members, asking them the following questions:

1. Who are you? What work do you do?
2. What do you like most about your work?
3. How would you notice tomorrow that this day has been useful to you and the team?

The second question aims at giving team members the opportunity to talk about positive aspects of work. Within 5 minutes, all team members talk about things that are important to them, things they enjoy and they are proud of. This provides a good platform to talk about their answers to question 3, which often is a difficult question when people are problem focused.

In response to question 3, people at first have a tendency to talk about things they do not want—things that go wrong. For example, team members start talking about everything their team manager does wrong. Listening to microprogression is a very important skill. A team member will say something like this: "Everybody is fed up; nobody wants this." This comment is an example of microprogression. It is a negative comment, which has a positive opposite to it because if nobody wants it like it is now, what does everybody want it to become?

A solution-focused intervention to this microprogression is, "Yes, I certainly understand nobody wants the situation to stay like this. Suppose this day has helped to change things for the better, how would you notice that?" In a team of eight, the likelihood for one member to come up with a useful answer is quite high. When six team members say they don't know, but one says he has some ideas about a better future, this changes the focus of the conversation and helps everybody to start to expect that a positive change is possible.

Often, when people start talking about how they would like things to be, small examples of previous successes are mentioned. For example, if one team member says, "The last couple of weeks, the team manager tried a bit harder," then this is enough to build on. The solution-focused coach might respond like this: "What did you notice that went better the last couple of weeks?"

Some team members will have examples; others might stay silent and just listen to what their colleagues see that they don't see (yet). The solution-focused coach writes down the positive examples on a flip chart and responds with modest enthusiasm to positive examples. It is important not to be too enthusiastic in response to small examples of improvements because, if the solution-focused coach is more positive than the team members, they will feel that the coach is trying to convince them. When people feel someone is trying to convince them, a reactive response will occur. This means that people will try to regain their freedom by not agreeing with the coach.

After a patient and lengthy inquiry regarding what went a bit better the last couple of weeks, the solution-focused coach can ask the following question: "Ah, I understand small things are a bit better the last couple of weeks. You will not want to lose those small improvements, I assume. So, can you tell me what doesn't have to change? What is going well enough?" This intervention leads to more and more examples of what works well. People describe the desired future and start to prepare themselves for this desired future. The solution-focused coach can ask, "What would be the benefit of this desired future for the team?"

A team session like this will take about an hour. At the end of the team session, the solution-focused coach may well ask the team members, "Will you please think about what you can do to help make the session with the team manager useful?" This intervention is called the *interval intervention*. This means that people are not pressed to give a constructive answer straightaway, but instead they get time to let the question sink in and form their answers in their minds.

SESSION WITH THE TEAM MANAGER

The session with the team manager follows a similar structure to the one with the team members. This session is a preparation for the team manager to reach a mind-set in which he is expecting to and willing to achieve positive outcomes with the team. To help him reach this mind-set, it is important to acknowledge his perspective, to normalize his situation, to explore how he has been coping, and to let him describe which positive changes he wants to achieve and when things were already a bit better in the past. After getting his authorization and changing a few details to protect the client's privacy, here goes: Create a positive expectation. The following interventions can be used to achieve this:

- Short acknowledging interventions
  - I understand.
  - That must be hard.
  - Sounds logical. Can you tell me a bit more about this please?
  - I understand that that must be hard!
- Normalising
  - Yes, I guess lots of people would find that hard.
  - Yes, that is completely understandable.
  - Yes, that makes sense/is logical.
  - Of course this is not what you want.
  - I can understand you want to change that. I can imagine you would like that to be different.
- Leap frogging/jumping over a problem
  - Suppose the problem is solved, what will be better then?
  - Suppose the problem is solved, how would you notice that?
  - What is the first thing that would tell you the problem has gone?
- Focus on what the client wants to change
  - What is it that you would like to change?
  - What do you appreciate about the team? What works well? What would you like to keep how it is now?
  - What do you want to be different? What would you like to be different?
- Exploring the desired success for the client
  - What would you like to achieve?
  - What would you want instead of (the problem)?
  - How would you like things to be different?
  - How would you like the situation to become?
  - What would you want the future situation to look like?
  - What could you do when the problem was solved?

SESSION WITH TEAM MANAGER AND
TEAM MEMBERS TOGETHER

The next step is to facilitate a session with both the team members and the team manager. It is important to help them to stay focused on the positive outcomes they are looking for. The solution-focused coach helps to achieve this by letting the team members and the team manager talk about the desired future and the positive changes, however small, that have already been achieved. Very often, arguing parties want to achieve the same positive future. Nobody likes to work in a negative environment and everybody wants to have a good time at work. The solution-focused coach can help them see all the things they all want to happen. The coach summarizes what everybody wants to achieve (consensus intervention) like this: "You all want to leave the past behind and to move forward to become a better team. How would you notice you are becoming a better team?"

The solution-focused coach constantly explores what the desired future looks like, what works to achieve that desired future, and what the benefit would be of achieving the desired future for everybody. Interventions that are useful are summarized next:

- Exploring the desired success from a different perspective
  - How would others notice that the problem is solved?
  - How would others notice things are better?
- Clarifying the positive results/benefits of the desired future
  - What will be the benefit of that?
  - What will be better when you have achieved that?
  - Ah, I can imagine that's what you all want to achieve!
- Clarifying the positive results/benefits of the desired future from a different perspective
  - What would it bring others?
  - How would it help others?
- Exploring previous successes and positive exceptions
  - When were things (a bit) better?
  - When was the problem a bit less bad?
  - When did the team manage a bit better to…?
  - What was different then? What was better then?
  - What did you all do to make that happen?
  - Interesting…how did that help?
- Exploring previous successes and positive exceptions from another perspective
  - What would xxx say if I asked him when things were already a bit better?

- How would xxx have been able to notice things were a bit better then?
- Which situations would xxx mention that went better?
- What would xxx have noticed when things went better?
- How would xxx say that success happened?
- On which point of the scale would xxx say you were when things were better?
- Defining one step forward
  - Is this useful?
  - How is it useful to you?
  - How can you use this?
  - What ideas do you come up with that will take you one step forward?
  - What would be the first sign that would tell you that you are moving in the right direction?
  - Which small step could you take tomorrow?
- One step forward from another perspective
  - Who would notice your step first?
  - Who would notice your success first?
  - What would xxx say one step forward would look like?

CONCLUSION

Focusing on microprogression in conflict resolution is a key intervention because it acknowledges small and subtle changes toward a more constructive mind-set in people. This acknowledgement encourages people to move forward and to shift from problem-focused talk to talking about which positive outcomes they want to achieve.

17

REDUCING PERSONNEL TURNOVER
RATE FROM 50 TO 10%

Paolo Terni

At the end of 2005, I was approached by a leading tractor manufacturer. They wanted help in solving a problem: the very high turnover rate of their youngest and brightest employees. Of the 15 young college graduates with management potential who were hired in the previous 12 months, eight had left the company, snatched up by other businesses and corporations. *How could they stop bleeding talent?*

A SOLUTION-FOCUSED APPROACH

We decided then not to pursue a problem-solving approach, but rather to follow a solution-focused approach. It did not matter why those eight left. What mattered is that others stayed. We might never know why those who left chose to do so; each one probably had his or her own personal reasons. After all, pay and benefits in the company were in line with the appropriate benchmarks. Furthermore, my client was a very desirable employer (the company offered good international career opportunities in a high-tech field in rural Italy, where there are no big businesses).

We do know, however, how to help people choose to stay: the secret is to involve them in their own career development. The client identified 37 people as being particularly talented who, at the same time, were at risk of being offered tempting deals by other businesses. We decided to ask these 37 future managers and executives what kinds of activities would help them grow professionally. We decided to ask them what kind of work culture would be best conducive to their professional growth. We decided to ask them to co-create skills-development programs that would make full use of the company's assets. Here is how the program unfolded:

1. The first intervention was a very peculiar "assessment center": We watched participants perform certain tasks and then we talked about their signature strengths. We used questionnaires and then we talked about values and goals. We interviewed them one-by-one and we co-created unique self-development plans in what turned out to be brief coaching sessions. Mostly, we asked them how they could best grow in the company while helping the company grow. What kinds of behaviors and practices would make this company an interesting place to work? How could they make that happen? *The goal was to engage them to be active participants in creating the relationship patterns (i.e., the culture) that would characterize the company they would like to belong to.*

2. The second intervention involved outdoor team-building events, splitting participants into two groups on different weekends. That did a lot to strengthen their sense of belonging, and it did wonders to develop an informal network among the participants. Lastly, it fostered positive relationships and curiosity about each other's jobs, skills, and vision.

3. The third intervention was a 1-day brainstorming session with all the participants together. The format and the exercises were vintage solution focus. What works? What can we do to make it better? The participants came up with many interesting ideas that were, right there and then, developed into plans and work projects.

4. The fourth phase was not an intervention at all; it was the participants' taking the lead and implementing their ideas and plans. They organized monthly meetings where an executive would introduce his or her department. The participants who worked in the department featured during that month prepared and delivered a presentation about their work to the group as an introduction to the Q&A session with the executive. These 37 people took the lead for the celebrations for the 70th anniversary of the establishment of the company; they prepared materials and presentations, worked as guides for groups of visitors (schools, delegations, and so on), and worked side-by-side with

marketing to make the most of this milestone. They created special-interest groups online; they shared best practices while working together on interdepartmental projects; they organized visits to Expos. Our support was limited to a few brief coaching sessions here and there to coach executives or managers on how to best coach these young talents.

5. As a benefit and as an element of their professional growth, participants were invited to attend 2-day workshops on stress management, project management, and leadership.

6. Further exciting steps were planned for the next year: key interfunctional projects would be assigned to the participants; they would be responsible for introducing new knowledge to the company; a yearly retreat was in the final planning stages; some of them would also be coaching the newest hires!

Bottom line: by 2008, only 4 of the 37 had left since 2006; in 2008, the 12 newest "young talents" hired since the program began started the same program as the "second generation."

Obviously, this case study has no ambition of being scientific. We cannot attribute with certainty the dramatic drop in turnover rate exclusively to our intervention; we cannot control the market's fluctuations and all the other factors that can lead people to make career choices. However, with the comfort of continuous feedback, I can say it is my belief that our intervention was part of the solution.

18

OPENING FOR BRIEF COACHING SESSIONS

Paolo Terni

CONTEXT

Coaching is a practice whose effectiveness has long been recognized in the business world; it is used to train leaders, to help managers perform, and to help employees solve problems and acquire new skills and competencies.

Executive coaching is the "purest" form of coaching that can be found in organizational settings. Executive coaching is usually not linked to any given performance goal or skill-development plan; often it is a benefit provided by the employer and the executive has the freedom to work on whatever issue he or she thinks is relevant at the moment.

Life coaching is also well established. People seek out a coach to help them figure out the solution to a specific personal or professional problem, to clarify their goals and values, to improve relationships, and to find a better balance in life.

Solution-focused brief coaching is gaining more and more attention in this economy, thanks to the magic word "brief." The promise of achieving the same results in less time while spending less money is very attractive to individual clients as well as businesses and corporations.

The opening I am presenting in this chapter can be used to introduce the first coaching session in brief coaching interventions aimed at private clients (solution-focused brief life coaching) and executives (solution-focused brief executive coaching).

BRIEF COACHING

Brief coaching is about being brief and effective at the same time. Everything that is said or that is asked by the coach needs to make a difference for the client. Even the introduction to the coaching session is an opportunity to have a positive impact on the client. This chapter will present one way to open the coaching conversation that will plant useful seeds with the client.

INTRODUCING A SOLUTION-FOCUSED BRIEF COACHING SESSION: GOAL NEGOTIATION

In brief coaching sessions, the first task[1] of the coach is to negotiate a goal for the session with the client. This is done using the following questions (Berg & Szabó, 2005):

1. To identify the issue the client would like to work on, use a question such as one of the following:
   - What needs to happen in our conversation today so that it will turn out to be really useful for you?
   - What would have to be different as a result of our meeting today for you to say that our talking was worthwhile?
   - What do you want to be different as a result of coming here?
2. To explore how the change they seek would be a solution for them, use a question such as one of the following:
   - And if we do that today, what will you be doing differently?
   - Suppose you were doing X. What would be different for you?
3. To explore how that change is a solution in their environment and in their system of relationships, use a question such as one of the following:
   - What would your boss see that would tell her that it was a good idea for you to come see me without your having to say it?
   - What would your co-worker do differently, once he notices that you have more confidence about yourself, without your having to say anything?
   - What would you do then?

4. To be sure we did not miss anything, the following question can be asked at any point in the discussion:
   • What else?

Solution-focused therapists might recognize the preceding protocol as an evolution of and adaptation to coaching of the protocol used in therapy by Insoo Kim Berg (Berg & Szabó, 2005), which was articulated the following way:

• Problem description: "How can I be of help to you?"
• Check how the issue is a problem for them: "How is this a problem for you?"
• Explore attempted solutions: "What have you tried in the past? Was it helpful?"

SPICING THINGS UP: PRESUPPOSITIONS

Now, many of the questions asked in brief coaching are rich in presuppositions. For example, asking the client who shows up for a follow-up session, "What is better?" presupposes that something is better. Additional presuppositions can easily be introduced in the previously listed goal-negotiation questions, for example, by using "when" instead of "suppose" or "if." Instead of asking, "Suppose you were doing X. What would be different for you?" the coach can ask, "When you do X, what will be different for you?" This question presupposes that the coachee will be doing X, where X is whatever the coachee would like to be doing (e.g., confronting her co-worker, being more organized, etc.). The fact that the client will be doing X is a given. The only thing to be clarified is what will be different then for the client.

I believe that another opportunity for the coach to introduce presuppositions in the coaching conversation is at the very beginning of the session, even before the goal-negotiation phase. In a quest to pack as much punch as possible in the 30 minutes or so I spend with clients, I have been using a "presupposition-laced" opening that introduces goal-negotiation questions during the first coaching session. The opening I use has the following structure:

1. An *introduction* that stresses the time constraint; the specific formulation depends on the way the practitioner operates. Here are a few examples:
   • Now, as you know, our session will last 30 minutes.

- Now, in 30 minutes you will hear a chime, and that is the signal that our session has come to a closing and we need to wrap it up.
- Now, we have 30 minutes for your coaching session.

2. The *core* message: "I don't know when you will find what you are looking for, whatever it is that you want to work on. It may be in the first 10 minutes of our conversation, or it may be in the first 20 minutes, or it may be at the very end of our conversation. You might even find it after you leave here! But 30 minutes is the time we have now for our conversation."

3. *Bridge* to the first question: "And that leads me to the first question I have for you: What needs to happen in our conversation today so that it will turn out to be really useful for you?"

The presupposition implicit in this opening is that the coachee will find what she or he is looking for during or after the session. That, we know. The only thing we don't know is when.

This opening was inspired by the patterns of indirect suggestions first explored by Milton Erickson. It can be seen as a combination of the pattern "all possibilities of a class of responses," which establishes a narrow frame of desirable possibilities within which whatever the client chooses is OK, and the pattern "presupposition, order of occurrence," which presupposes that the thing will happen and the only question is when (Sommer, 1992).

To maximize the usefulness of this opening, it is good to know the following:

- As with all indirect suggestion, a key success factor is the delivery. Pacing the client's breathing, the coach should talk slowly, in a calm tone of voice, while putting emphasis on key words and phrases—such as, "we *will* find"; "*here*"; "in the first *10 minutes*"; "in the *first* 20 minutes"; "at the very *end* of our conversation"; "after you *leave* here"—with a slight pause or a change in pitch, tone, tempo, or volume.
- The relevance of this opening is directly proportional to the time available for the coaching session. When the session is brief, this opening is very useful. When the coaching session is longer (1 hour or more), there are many more opportunities for the coach to do things that have a positive impact on the client during the session itself without having to use a carefully crafted opening.

CONTRAINDICATIONS

This opening is to be used when clients are showing up of their own free will (i.e., when they are the ones that will foot the bill for the coaching session). It is not to be used when working with mandated clients or when there are doubts about the client's being likely to establish a customer-type relationship (De Jong & Berg, 2007). I would not use this opening when working with managers or employees whose coaching is being paid for by the company.

The risk is that the question can backfire. A typical adverse reaction would be the following response: "I am not looking for anything; my boss sent me here." In those situations, time is better spent explaining to the coachee the overall context of the coaching intervention and then using a great deal of care in the goal-negotiation phase. That can be achieved by introducing other clients' points of view as frequently as possible and by using relationship questions such as "What do you suppose your boss would say needs to happen here so that she would think giving you this opportunity to be coached was a good idea?" "What would your co-workers say?"

I've also found that using this opening with executives is usually a safe bet. Even when the company is paying for their coaching, they are invested enough in the company itself to see it as a personal opportunity for growth.

I find this opening particularly useful during the first session. It helps set the tone of the coaching conversation and it is a nice way to remind the client of the time constraints while slipping in some suggestions. I would not use this in follow-up conversations, since the client already knows about the time constraint and it might sound inappropriate.

NOTE

1. After a few words are exchanged to establish rapport and context, the coach can use situational cues (e.g., the weather, how the trip was on the way there, etc.) to elicit a few remarks. The coach can also ask about the client's job with a focus on the positive and the intent to validate the coachee from the very beginning (e.g., the coach might say, "Head of R&D! That sounds great! What do you like most about your job?")

REFERENCES

Berg, I. K., & Szabó, P. (2005). *Brief coaching for lasting solutions.* New York: Norton.

De Jong, P., & Berg, I. K. (2007). *Interviewing for solutions.* Pacific Grove, CA: Brooks/Cole.

Sommer, C. (1992). *Conversational hypnosis: A manual of indirect suggestions.* Downers Grove, IL: Sommer Solutions, Inc.

19

A SOLUTION-FOCUSED HR PROFESSIONAL

Gwenda Schlundt Bodien

Is it possible for human resource (HR) professionals to achieve goals positively and quickly? For HR professionals, this can be a real challenge because they are often in a position in which they have to manage managers—and that can be a difficult job! The solution-focused approach can be of assistance and can help the HR professional to switch quickly between the different roles (coach, advisor, manager) that are required. How? That's the subject of this chapter.

The solution-focused approach is a respectful change approach that acknowledges problems, turns those problems into positive goals, finds internal solutions that fit the specific circumstances by analysing previous successes and positive exceptions to the problem, and reaches those positive goals step by step. The approach works well, research indicates. This is reasonably easy to understand in circumstances where someone wants to help someone else with a problem—for example, in coaching and therapy.

But HR professionals are not helping others only. Sometimes helping others doesn't get the job done. If the rule applies that all managers should hand in their performance appraisal by the first of November so that the HR department is able to estimate the total cost of bonuses and pay raises, and a manager doesn't comply because he doesn't feel it is a problem to be late, then maybe helping this manager with a problem he doesn't perceive he has is not the best way forward. Nobody can be helped against his own wish. HR professionals have their own goals, including the goals of the organisation, to achieve.

How can the solution-focused approach be used in circumstances where it is not so much about helping people to define their own goals but rather about directing someone to achieve organisational goals? Gwenda Schlundt Bodien and Coert Visser developed a model based on the solution-focused approach for these sorts of situations (see Figure 19.1). When the goals of the organisation or the goals of the HR professional prevail, solution-focused directing (as we call it) is in order. Human resource professionals clarify the positive results expected of the manager. The organisational goals are the central point of focus of the conversation.

The "leading from behind" posture only partly applies now. The HR professional is leading as far as the goals are concerned. The HR professional doesn't ask the manager what his goals are, but tells him what is expected. However, a not-knowing posture does apply with regard to the solutions that fit the manager best. The HR professional asks how the manager is going to reach the goals and doesn't instruct him how to achieve them. The focus is on finding internal solutions.

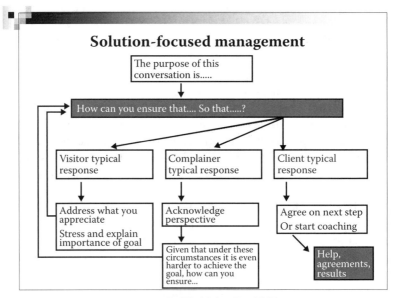

© 2009 – Schlundt Bodien & Visser - NOAM

Figure 19.1 Solution-focused directing format.

As with solution-focused coaching, the basic attitude is inviting, encouraging, goal-oriented, future focused, and activating. A solution-focused directing conversation combines friendliness with clarity, and understanding with determination. This can be hard, especially when the HR professional gets annoyed with delaying behaviour of a manager. Preparation helps to keep the conversation goal oriented and to prevent sidetracks or escalations and arguments.

PREPARING FOR A SOLUTION-FOCUSED DIRECTING CONVERSATION

Solution-focused directing requires that the "director" be mandated by the organisation to act in this role. What does the HR professional expect of the manager and what is a good reason to expect this? The HR professional prepares by answering the following questions:

1. What is the goal of the conversation?
2. What do I expect and what is my good reason to expect this of the manager?
3. When do I expect my goals to be achieved by the manager and what is my good reason to keep this time scale?
4. What do I appreciate with regard to this manager? (And when has he already shown the desired behaviour?)

The answers to these questions provide the HR professional with a solid basis for directing sentences. These directing sentences are built on two pillars:

- WHAT does the HR professional expect?
- WHICH positive results will be achieved if the manager fulfils the expectations?

Because the goal is a given but the solutions are found by the manager himself, the directing sentences are being phrased as a question: *How can you ensure that...so that...?* Of course, there are many different ways in which the directing questions can be formulated. The pillars stay the same: the WHAT you expect and the TO WHICH END you expect this.

VISITOR-TYPICAL, COMPLAINER-TYPICAL, AND CLIENT-TYPICAL RESPONSES

However well prepared HR professionals are, they can't control the way managers respond. Managers typically can respond in three different ways: A visitor-typical response would be when the manager tells the HR professional that he doesn't want to talk about the planning of the performance appraisals because he is too busy and doesn't find that topic very interesting. A complainer-typical response would be when the manager says that he knows that he is late, but he can't help it because of various reasons. A client-typical response would be when the manager says that he understands he has to be on time and he wants to be on time, and he comes up with solutions to meet the deadlines or he asks the HR professional to help him with his planning problem.

HR professionals respond differently to each type of interaction. To a visitor-typical response of the manager, an appropriate response is one of understanding and with a friendly determination to stick to the goal of the conversation. At a certain point, the manager will start to understand the topic is not going to go away. He may become a bit more agitated because he now understands he will have to deal with it, so he uses a complainer-typical response.

To a complainer-typical response, the HR professional responds with acknowledgement and by understanding the complaints without letting the complaints be a reason not to achieve the goal. "Given that your business unit is under a lot of strain, which makes it even harder for you to meet the deadline, what are your ideas to make sure you will meet the performance appraisal deadline so that our management team is provided with the necessary financial reports on time?"

The manager is likely to keep complaining for awhile, but will soon understand that his problems are being acknowledged yet the goal keeps on being stressed. At this point, a client-typical interaction develops. The manager agrees with the goal. He might ask the HR professional for support, in which case the HR professional can switch from directing to coaching.

Figure 19.1 shows a format for a solution-focused directing conversation in which the manager notices:

1. The goals of the HR professional/the organisation are stressed constantly.
2. The complaints of the manager are acknowledged and understood and listened to.
3. The contribution of the manager is appreciated and valued.

4. The manager himself is expected to take the next step to achieve the goals of the HR professional/the organisation.
5. The manager has the freedom and chance to find the solutions that fit him and are his own to achieve the goal.

The solution-focused approach is not an answer to all problems and doesn't make challenging situations in organisations' "pieces of cake." But the approach does very often help to know what you want to achieve vividly and to actually achieve those vivid goals.

20

RESILIENCY AND CHALLENGE

Liselotte Baeijaert and Anton Stellamans

BACKGROUND AND COMMENTS

This exercise was developed when we were hosting resilience workshops in different organisations. The idea of working with a graph on the floor was presented to us in a workshop organised by Outward Bound. We changed the parameters of the graph and added the coaching part in pairs after the group discussion. We developed a framework on resilience and collected useful questions about resilience. People we worked with have found this exercise uplifting and interesting. The activity is solution focused:

- Participants are treated as the experts of their own learning and learning goals.
- They focus on their goals and resources.
- They are invited to make a first step toward a desired goal.
- They can show mutual appreciation and encourage the others of the group.

TECHNICAL REQUIREMENTS

The room: big enough room with chairs in a circle. If there is a green and suitable outdoor environment, make use of it!

Material and preparation: Give a short presentation about resilience. Make a graph on the floor by means of ropes or tape. Indicate the parameters of the axes. Provide coloured cards

85

(two different colours: one colour for the current situation and one for the preferred situation) to write their names on. Prepare enough cards with solution-focused questions, one for each pair of participants.

WHAT HAPPENS IN THE EXERCISE?

The people who do this exercise are asked to assess their current resiliency levels and their current (work) challenge levels varying from 1 to 10 on the resilience axis and 1 to 10 on the challenge axis. These are put in a grid formed by the two axes on the floor. With this exercise, the resilience and engagement of the group become tangible and therefore more manageable as the preferred situation of the group becomes visible.

Sometimes there is a clear correlation between resilience and challenge. This happens when people discover that they need more challenges to improve their resilience. More challenges mean more possibilities to fail and to learn from these difficulties. Other participants report they want fewer challenges in order to feel more resilient. Too many changes have undermined their capacity to bounce back and see the meaningfulness of it all. In still other cases, participants are happy with their current levels of challenge in the team but realise that they can become more resilient by working on their capacity to learn from their experiences, for example. Other variables can be explored in a coaching conversation to help participants to find out how they can improve their capacity to react in a more resilient way or to discover at which time in their job they felt more resilient.

When the positions are clarified, the team exchanges what they discovered about the current team resilience and the tendency for change (more or fewer challenges wanted). After that, pairs can coach one another with solution-focused questions in order to find out what works and what doesn't, to describe what would be different in the preferred situation, what worked perhaps better in the past, and to find out what would be a first small step to make progress in the direction of the wish.

21

COACHING FOR RESILIENCE

Liselotte Baeijaert and Anton Stellamans

WHAT IS THIS EXERCISE ABOUT?

This is a team-coaching exercise that can be done during a longer team development programme or in a one-on-one coaching. It explores the resilience of team members individually and the possible relationship between resilience and current challenges at work.

Resiliency has become a key concept in today's quickly changing and challenging world. We define resilience as the capacity to deal with challenges, bounce back from difficulties, adapt to changes, and to learn from these experiences. It is also the art of tapping into resources, successes, and everything that creates energy and enthusiasm in one's life and work.

We see a very obvious link between solution-focused (SF) therapy/ coaching and resilience. As SF therapists and coaches, we respect the expertise of our clients and assume that they know best their problems as well as they know best which solutions could work for them. Our SF conversation, presence, and questions support and feed this client capacity of resilience to take control over their own lives and progress. Clients and coachees have found the concept of resilience very useful and like to spend time thinking and exchanging ideas about what makes them more resilient.

The meaning of resilience shows resemblance with concepts like self-management, adaptability, the art of living wisely, energy management, personal balance. It is however, distinct from all these. A high energy level, for example, will often influence one's resiliency. It seems clear that having a lot of energy and physical strength will make it easier for people to deal with difficulties. On the other hand, it is perfectly possible to feel very resilient and yet have very little physical energy. A good explanation of the meaning of resilience is therefore useful when doing this exercise.

FRAME

Time: allow for 1.5 to 2 hours to do the complete activity in a useful way.
The activity is suitable for 6 to 20 people.

PURPOSE AND PRACTICAL EFFECT

Doing this exercise in a team development programme or team coaching can lead to a better understanding of resilience. It sheds a light on the needs and personal experiences and wisdom of co-workers; it can enhance buddy coaching, deepen mutual support, and might lead to a revision or switch of tasks, roles, and perhaps functions. It makes people more aware of the variety and resources in the team and it invites people to connect better and have useful conversations.

PREPARATION

1. Create a graph on the floor, using cords or ropes. The horizontal axis represents the scale of challenges. Indicate "little challenge" at the left side and "lots of challenge" at the right side. The vertical axis represents the scale of resilience. Indicate "not at all resilient" at the bottom and "very resilient" at the top.
2. Prepare two cards in two different colours for each participant.
3. Write down a set of solution-focused questions for your participants to help them with the "buddy coaching."

DETAILED DESCRIPTION

Ask your participants what they know about the concept of resilience. What in their view typifies resilient people? And what is the contrary of resilient people? How is resilience important for their work and life? You might then give a short lecture about resilience. This will help your participants to understand resilience and give themselves a score on the scale. This is what you can tell them:

Resilience has become a key concept in today's quickly changing world. It is the power that people need to adapt swiftly to what happens to them and to the contexts they operate in, to make their life and work meaningful, and to move forward to whatever they define as success. Resilient people understand the art of accepting the things they cannot change. They don't waste energy in complaining or in producing useless arguments, nor do they fight the "do not fight" reality. Instead, they cooperate with whatever emerges in the here and now situation—successes as well as difficulties and setbacks. They keep their eyes in the direction of the future possibilities and the small steps they can take in order to move forward. The acronym A.R.M.S. can help you to remember the concept of resilience further. Resilient people are ARMED to deal well with change and difficulties:

Accept: they accept what is happening, even if it is difficult, hard, or painful.

Reconnect: they reconnect to what helps them move forward, their sources of success, their solutions, and the people around them.

Meaningful: they build meaningful stories about their life now and about their goals and preferred situation.

Step: they keep moving forward with small steps in the direction of their preferred situation.

Help your participants to assess their own resilience. You can suggest the following:

If you want to assess your own resilience you can start asking yourself three basic questions:

1. How well, on a scale from 1 to 10, are you able to deal with and overcome difficulties and setbacks in your work? A 10 means you succeed in doing this all the time in the best possible way. A 1 means the complete opposite. (Explain that scaling is subjective and personal but is also helpful to manage progress.)

2. On a scale from 1 to 10, how well are you able to reflect upon what happened and learn from that? A 10 means you always reflect on what happened and learn from that in the best possible way and a 1 means the exact opposite.

3. On a scale from 1 to 10, how well are you able to connect to yourself and other people, enjoy what you do and what you have, think positively, tap into the successes and cheerful events of your work, feel happy with yourself and your working conditions? A 10 means you do this all the time at the maximum and a 1 means the exact opposite. Once you have answered these questions, you can give yourself an overall scale on resilience.

Assessing your challenges on a scale is also a purely subjective matter. "Lots of challenge" for one person can mean little challenge for another. Give a score on how you experience the challenges in your work today. A 10 means the maximum stretch possible and a 1 means the minimum challenge you can imagine. (Give some time to your participants to think about the scores on the scale that apply to them today.)

Participants then receive two small (preferably round) cards in two different colours and are asked to write their names on both cards. You invite them to put one of their cards (e.g., the red one) on the floor at the place where the values of both axes meet; this is their current position. Next, invite them to lay down the second card on the position where they want to be (their preferred situation). Normally, they move up (more resilience) on the vertical axis and more to the left or the right on the horizontal axis, which respectively means less challenge or more challenge. It is also possible that they move straight up on the vertical axis or that they don't move at all, which means they are happy with their current position. You can give them thin pieces of thread now to link their current and their preferred positions. On the floor, you now see a two-dimensional representation of the resilience/challenge of the team. Invite the team members to take a close look at the overall picture and ask them what they see. Host a constructive dialogue about what they notice.

After a short exchange with the full team, invite them to pair up and to coach one another with the help of solution-focused questions. The goal of the exercise is to have a useful conversation with your colleagues, exploring what creates and improves resilience at work. Suggest that they find a comfortable place or go for a short walk if time and space allow it. Give them 30 minutes for this and indicate when the first 15 minutes have passed, inviting them to switch roles. If they are not acquainted with solution-focus you might give them the following questions on a small piece of paper.

SOME SOLUTION-FOCUSED RESILIENCE QUESTIONS

- Can you tell me where you are on the graph?
- What challenges are you pleased with in your work?
- What do you do already to act with resilience?
- What is helpful for you already?
- Please tell me about the spot where you want to be. What is different there?
- What would you notice that is different there?
- What would other people notice about you when you would be there?
- What could you do already to move a little to that position?
- What might other people do to help you?
- What difference would that make to your work and life?

Invite the participants back into the group and ask for what they have learned in this short exercise:

- What did you learn?
- What worked well in your conversation?
- How was this useful for you?
- What is one idea you want to bring into practice?
- What else do you take home?
- What did you learn about resilience?

You can close this exercise by asking participants to give the person they worked with a compliment about something that struck them in a positive way.

22

STRENGTH-BASED SCHOOL MEETINGS

Jay Trenhaile

Meetings to discuss the progress or behavior of a student as well as the development of an individualized educational program (IEP) are often a challenging time for parents, teachers, and the student. These meetings may involve discussion of a variety of both positive and negative topics; however, they are often stressful for participants. This is true even for teachers who understand the educational system, but have a child within the "system." The high stress levels are often a direct result of the meetings' becoming focused on problems and activities that the child does wrong, especially when behavior and academic effort are discussed. Understandably, when a meeting does turn negative or problem focused, the parent and student often leave frustrated and may develop negative feelings toward the school, teachers, and staff members.

Research conducted by Pruitt, Wandry, and Hollums (1998) found families with a child receiving special education have strong opinions about improving interaction with teachers. For example, 23% of parents interviewed reported that educators could be more responsive to needs of families by improving the quality and quantity of communication. Similarly, 27% of parents reported that educators could be more sensitive by listening to them. The authors advocated a solutions-building approach to conducting school-based meetings and developed the strength-based school meetings (SBSM) approach, modeled from a protocol developed by De Jong and Berg (2007) when working with clients.

Appropriate modifications are made to provide a structured, strength-based approach for use within the context of typical school meetings.

STARTING THE MEETING—STAGE 1

First, at the start of the school meeting, the purpose or goal(s) should be discussed. Shortly after this introduction, the student and parent must be given an opportunity to discuss their view of the current situation. Careful attention should be paid toward exceptions to the child's problem and small successes that are exhibited. In addition, within this stage, the student and parent must feel as though their statements and perceptions have been understood and heard. Okun's (1992) research suggested that clients often rely on nonverbal behaviors as a means of examining whether they are "heard" or not. Certainly, many other basic communication skills are important and useful beyond nonverbal behaviors during the initial stages of the meeting and professional jargon should be avoided.

Following parent and student comments, teachers and other school staff members should be allowed to respond to the current state of affairs. During stage 1, the facilitator must be cautious of parents, teachers, and students who lose their focus and move conversations away from the purpose of the meeting. Redirection back to the topic should be handled carefully by using statements such as, "How are you involved in the situation?" rather than debating statements or allowing for lengthy problem-focused discussions. In most cases, stage 1 of the meeting should last no longer than 10–15 minutes with minimum discussion of the "problem," especially because participants are generally well informed about the issue being addressed.

INVESTIGATION OF EXCEPTIONS—STAGE 2

A simple introductory phrase such as, "What are some things that we know Johnny does well?" is an excellent way to start the focus on strengths. This question is often followed by, "How did Johnny get to be so good in these classes?" and "In what classes does Johnny get passing grades and what is his behavior in these subjects?"—successful follow-up questions that keep the focus positive. All responses should be recognized as potential strengths and interests that can be utilized within the educational system. For example, if it is stated that Johnny does well in a certain activity such as basketball, then that interest and strength should be exploited. By focusing Johnny's educational assignments on this topic, the team is providing him an opportunity to complete academic requirements in a specific area of interest. This could easily include subjects such as reading, math, and writing about basketball.

After the first question is asked, responses may indicate exceptions to the problems Johnny exhibits. This makes the problem seem more manageable because it is not occurring all the time. It also points out possible steps toward a desired state.

After allowing for adequate responses to the first question, the second question elicits a strength-based perception of a potentially problematic area. The question can be initiated by the facilitator's asking team members to respond to the following: "What activities do we know that Johnny does but needs to do more often?" Answers often help determine short-term goals, which are useful when completing an IEP.

After the formulation of short-term goals, a version of scaling questions (Berg, 1994; Berg & de Shazer, 1993; Berg & Miller, 1992; de Shazer, 1988) can be used. The applications for scaling in SBSM have many possibilities during stage 2. First, the student's, teachers', and parents' confidence in the program and the short-term objectives that have been developed should be scaled.

After this, further questions can be utilized to increase confidence. For example, "On a scale of 1 to 10 with 1 being not at all and 10 being good enough, how confident are you that progress toward these goals will be made?" This question can be asked of all participants. The facilitator generally follows the confidence question with another question such as, "What would it take for you to move your confidence in this plan up a point or two on the scale?" A question such as this often elicits the respondent to discuss identifiable, concrete steps toward goal attainment. De Jong and Berg (2007) believe that clients' strengths can be reinforced through scaling motivation and confidence both by the facilitator and the clients themselves.

Following the discussion of short-term goals, the facilitator asks committee members to discuss activities related to long-term goals. For example, the facilitator may prompt participants with the question, "What do we need to see Johnny do that we are not sure he has the ability to do?" Information shared during this discussion then becomes the long-term goal(s) for the student.

CLOSURE—STAGE 3

The end of the meeting will best be focused on a feedback approach, which has been strongly advocated by de Shazer and colleagues (de Shazer, Berg, Lipchik, Nunnally, et al., 1986). The main methods of feedback advocated in SBSM are complimenting and task assignment.

By complimenting the student and perhaps parent, the sense of listening carefully is communicated (De Jong & Berg, 2007). Finishing a meeting on a positive note is critical to school meetings. Parents and students must leave meetings with a sense of being heard and an understanding that plans developed have been built around strengths of the student.

Task assignments are automatically built into any IEP as short- and long-term goals are formulated. These tasks are easily extracted by discussing specific steps needed to reach those goals. Because the task assignments have been discussed prior to the closure of the meeting, they merely need to be restated at this point.

In the case of follow-up meetings, the focus should still be directed toward continued use of client strengths. Scaling questions are also important during follow-up meetings. The current status of an individual's progress in school or specific academic or behavior areas can easily be scaled by teachers, parents, and students themselves. This may be asked by the question, "On a scale of 0 to 10, with 0 being not at all and 10 being good enough, how is school going?" The usefulness of scaling questions can be significant to educators. Berg reported that scaling provides an insight to individual awareness of many areas including "self-esteem, self-confidence, investment in change, willingness to work hard to bring about desired changes, prioritizing of problems to be solved, perception of hopefulness, and evaluation of progress" (1994, pp. 102–103).

REFERENCES

Berg, I., & de Shazer, S. (1993). Making numbers talk: Language in therapy. In S. Friedman (Ed.), *The new language of change: Constructive collaboration in psychotherapy* (pp. 5–23). New York: Guilford.

Berg, I., & Miller, S. (1992). *Working with the problem drinker.* New York: Norton.

Berg, I. K. (1994). *Family based services: A solution-focused approach.* New York: Norton.

De Jong, P., & Berg, I. K. (2007). *Interviewing for solutions* (3rd ed.). Belmont, CA: Thomson Brooks/Cole Publishing.

de Shazer, S. (1988). *Clues: Investigating solutions in brief therapy.* New York: Norton.

de Shazer, S., Berg, I., Lipchik, E., Nunnally, E., Molnar, A., Gingerich, W., et al. (1986). Brief therapy: Focused-solution development. *Family Process, 25*, 207–222.

Okun, B. F. (1992). *Effective helping: Interviewing and counseling techniques* (4th ed.). Pacific Grove, CA: Brooks/Cole.

Pruitt, P., Wandry, D., & Hollums, D. (1998). Listen to us! Parents speak out about their interactions with special educators. *Preventing School Failure, 42*(4), 161–162.

PROTOCOL FOR STRENGTH-BASED SCHOOL MEETINGS

Stage 1
- How are things going for Johnny?

Stage 2
- What are some things that we know Johnny does well?
    1. How did Johnny get to be so good in these classes?
    2. What classes does Johnny get passing grades in and what is his behavior in these subjects?
- What activities do we know Johnny does, but he needs to do them more often? [short-term goals]
- On a scale of 1 to 10, with 1 being not at all and 10 being good enough, how confident are you that progress toward these goals can be made?
- What would it take for you to move your confidence in this plan up a point or two on the scale?
- What do we need to see Johnny do that we are unsure if he has the ability to do? [long-term goals]

Stage 3
- Johnny has a number of strengths, including...
- These are some of the things we want Johnny to do more often before we meet again...

23

RESPONDING TO BULLYING IN PRIMARY SCHOOLS

Sue Young

In the day-to-day rough and tumble of school life, just as in the work-place, sometimes relationships become difficult and a pattern of behav-iour emerges that is unhelpful and can be hurtful. In a minority of cases, bullying can get serious, to the extent that it makes a child so unhappy that she or he becomes isolated in school and shows signs of stress at home such as wetting the bed, becoming suddenly moody and aggres-sive, or having unexplained aches and pains, particularly on school mornings. Children are reluctant to tell adults when they feel that they are being bullied. This may be because they are afraid that if they do, any action taken to stop it will make it worse. There are probably other, more complicated and subtle reasons, maybe very good reasons, to keep it quiet. So if adults want to help, they need to intervene gently.

One way to change this pattern of behaviour effectively, without entering into an investigative process that could be worrying to the child and may ultimately prove unhelpful, is to set up a solution-focused peer support group. The term "bullying" is not mentioned during this inter-vention because it is implicitly judgemental and possibly contentious.

The adult who will be leading the intervention interviews the child who is struggling in school and asks about his or her peer group:

- Who are you finding difficult?
- Who are your friends?
- Who else is around when things are difficult in school?

The children named by the child will make up the support group. From experience, a group of about five to eight children works nicely. There is no need to ask anything at all about what has been happening; indeed, this could be positively unhelpful. The lead person tells the child that the group is going to be asked to help out and makes an arrangement to see the child again in about a week, when it is expected that things will be a lot better.

The lead person gathers the named children together for a meeting straightaway without the supported child present and tells them the aim of the group: "I know you can all help me. I want your help to make [name] happier in school." No reasons are given why the child is unhappy. If it is felt that there needs to be any justification for the request, then the lead person can say, "We want everyone to be happy coming to this school, don't we?" Then the group members are asked to suggest how they might help in any small way to make the child needing support happier over the next week.

As each member of the group makes a suggestion, it is written down and repeated in the child's own words: For example, "Michael, you will talk to him/her at break-times…what a good idea! That will be great, Michael, thank you so much. I'm sure that will help make him/her happier!" Writing the idea down, repeating it with the child's name, and giving compliments all validate the idea and make it more likely to happen.

Someone in the group who cannot think of a new idea can be asked if he or she wants to choose to join in with someone else's. The lead person makes no suggestions, does not ask for any promises, and does not ask the group to be friends with the child. Once all the group members have come up with suggestions, the ideas are all repeated and complimented as the group's plan. Arrangements are made to see the group again after a week so that they can talk about how they are getting on.

A week later the child is seen again to find out "what's better." Usually, everything is fine and the child can be complimented on his or her part in whatever has been mentioned—for example,

"Michael's been playing with me at break-times."
"You have been playing with Michael at break-time! That's great! What else have you been doing that's making you happier now?"

Immediately after seeing the child being supported, the group review meeting takes place. The children are asked how they think it is going and what they have managed to do. Everyone who mentions something is complimented—for example,

"Who else has managed to do something?"

"I've been having my lunch with her."

"That's kind of you! Do you think that has helped make her happier?"

"Yes, she's happier now."

"That's excellent—well done for thinking of that!"

There is no need to check back against their suggestions from the week before or insist that everyone should have something to say. They can all be congratulated as a group for helping make the supported child happier in school. If necessary, depending on what they say, another meeting can be arranged—all of them will be keen to carry on.

When parents have made a complaint on behalf of their child about bullying, they need to be kept informed throughout and asked for their input about what they have noticed that tells them their child is becoming happier at school.

Reviewing a total of 50 cases when I used this approach, in 40 cases (80%), any difficulties the child was having stopped immediately after one group meeting. In a further 7 cases (14%), the group continued to meet up to 5 times before it was entirely successful. In 3 cases (6%), although the situation improved, the supported child continued with longer term input of individual SFBT.

Many other people have used this approach successfully at the first attempt, without any previous training in solution-focused work, showing that it is an accessible and practical strategy for school staff to use. More information can be found in Young (2009).

REFERENCE

Young, S. (2009). *Solution-focused schools: Anti-bullying and beyond.* London: BT Press.

24

SOLUTION FOCUS IN UK SCHOOLS
One Therapist's Practice

Paul Avard

I have used the attributes of the solution-focused approach as a counsellor/therapist and as a means of living my life in the best way I can for about 20 years now. It is to my eternal shame that I didn't fully recognise what I was doing in the early days—it just seemed natural to me that we treated those with whom we were involved with helping in a way that acknowledged their ownership of the issue or problem and, consequent to that, their ownership of the solution to the issue or problem, which they might well have arrived at with us helping them co-create a different, preferred reality. What I did on a day-to-day work or life basis didn't have a name; it was just how it was…

Then, after many years of working in this what I now recognise as intuitive way, I was invited to a two and a half day training session jointly run by a colleague in my service and a consultant paediatric psychologist. The topic was on a way of working with troubled adolescents using something called "solution-focused brief therapy." Talk about hand and glove: I began to see that what I had been doing—true, in an untrained way, and also because it suited me—had a genesis, a history, and a focus. It's a cliché, but I was "home" and what I did in the workplace now had a developing body of research, practice, and fellow practitioners. As Insoo would have said, "WOWW"!

Why "wow?" In the early years of my work as an advisory behaviour support teacher—as now, working for a specialist support service in a medium sized city in England's West Midlands (central area)—I had been supporting a sizeable cohort of the unteachable and frequently untouchable adolescent population that has become more and more marginalised and subcultural over the past several decades. Partly as a result of a target-led educational system and partly as a result of what Durkheim called "anomie"—"a condition where social and/or moral norms are confused, unclear, or simply not present." Durkheim felt that "this lack of norms—or preaccepted limits on behaviour in a society—led to deviant behaviour" (Perry, n.d.).

My career in the service for which I still work began by my supporting young people in what was a local authority secure unit. In essence, this was a 24/7 lock-up for troubled and troubling teenagers—with the occasional 11- or 12-year-old being placed for a short period of time. The young people were offered education and counselling and other support whilst on placement and the centre was staffed by social workers, not warders.

The majority of the young adults I worked with had come into contact with the legal and social care systems for a variety of reasons. On the one hand, we had a population of 12-year-old prostitutes and "rent boys," teenage murderers and rapists, profound and persistent burglars, habitual car thieves (in one case, over 400 offences!), and other felons. On the other hand, we had the victims, including the prostitutes and rent boys: children who had been severely sexually and emotionally abused, gang victims, young drug addicts and "mules," and youngsters who were beyond the care and control of their parents in so many other ways—the list went on and on. And it was here that I learned to give these young people credit for their lives' not being worse and for the majority having a place they'd rather be and not simply not being locked up in and with their lives.

I guess we did a reasonable job because the norm was for the young people to be brought in kicking and screaming and, then, following on from their time with us, for them to leave kicking and screaming because they didn't want to go—not because we had made them dependent upon us but because we worked with them to validate them as human beings.

I began to recognise that what I did then was solution focused: It had a name, wow!, and as I have moved through my trainings over the last several years—including time spent with BRIEF, among others—my work has changed and now I no longer work with such a small audience. I am out in mainstream education with a much larger cohort of students and families, teachers, and school management teams, as well as run major solution-focused training programs within our education authority and at national conferences.

I believe the work of Yasmin Ajmal and Harvey Ratner (Yasmin formerly of BRIEF and Harvey still with BRIEF) is very important; both have worked in mainstream and special schools to support those who needed help. In fact, Yasmin's books, *Solution Focused Thinking in Schools* (Rhodes & Ajmal, 1995) and *Solutions in Schools* (Ajmal & Rees, 2001), are still seminal works. Much of what was written is still a source of inspiration to me, as is the work of my friend Rayya Ghul (co-author with Lucie Duncan and Sarah Mousley) in the book, *Creating Positive Futures, Solution Focused Recovery From Mental Distress* (Duncan, Ghul, & Mousley, 2008).

The reason I suggest this is not just because these people are friends of mine; rather, it is because they believe that young people and those with trauma or recovering from trauma have the right and the skills to say that they want to change and how they want that change to look. In schools today in the UK, much of what goes on is about what is done to children—not by children. This isn't purely a condemnation of the school system or some off-handed political statement; more, it is a recognition that ignorance of the possible is going to get in the way of the actual. One of Yasmin's authors talks about solution-focused meetings in secondary schools (high school) where questions about the child are centred on "can do" rather than can't do (Harker as cited in Ajmal & Rees, 2001); for many, this is almost a revolutionary way of thinking even now in the twenty-first century.

Rayya's book is written from what is called an occupational therapy point of view, and Rayya and her colleagues join their academic and other skills together to show how the tasks we all normally associate with daily lives are fundamental to our sense of who and what we are. Making a cup of tea for some people is a challenge. For some of the kids I work with, attending class, behaving whilst in that class, and learning something from that class are all occupational demands made of them and, for a number of my clients, a challenge. And this may just be 0.01% of the issues that a cohort of close to 100 clients brings with it in my day-to-day work. The more we can help people see that the skills and resourcefulness they manage to bring to doing simple things are important, then, I believe, the more likely they are to discover that they have some control over what they might see as more significant aspects of their lives.

My practice, nowadays, is to help young people see that they can organise themselves to attend classes, and to behave in those classes and then to retain some of what they may well have learned by being in that class—and everything else that goes with being a student in a modern secondary school that makes high demands of all its students, or indeed, in a special school or an off-campus centre for the more challenging students.

Getting to class is microscopic when compared with some of the issues the young people I work with face, but it never ceases to amaze me that for some adults in school, this is the major reason for referral—that and defiance: the "make me" syndrome. So, I sit with the student and I sit with the teacher, classroom support, lunch-time supervisor, or whomever and we look at their day-to-day lives and how well they make the cup of tea of their lives. Gradually, they come to see that they can do what they need to do, and they get on and do it in the majority of cases.

Sometimes, kids don't want to see me, which is fine, and sometimes they self-refer; this may be because it gets them out of math or French. And sometimes, like with David (not his real name), seeing me is offered as an alternative to expulsion. This is not how I normally like to work, but the school is my client too because it pays for my time.

David arrived, listened to me as I explained my role and said he would stay and see the hour out. His preferred future was easy for him to outline: He didn't want to be in Mr X's class because of a clash of personality. When asked what he might do to make this future a reality, he expressed surprise and asked me whether I might not ask the head teacher to move him. I asked him if my doing the asking would be helpful. He suggested, after some reflection, that possibly he ought to express this as a possible solution himself. It would give him some time to talk to the management and let them hear him out. I agreed that this might be a way forward and after a little more chat we agreed to meet whenever (if) he were allowed back in school. David graduated at the end of 11th grade and gained some qualifications. It wasn't all plain sailing but at least he saw his time out and finished high school.

Is solution-focused brief therapy the answer to all adolescent or adult problems? "Probably not" would be the answer I'd give. Why? Largely, in my opinion, because a lot of people need to be trained to believe that they have a capacity to make a difference to their lives. People have become, it seems to me, almost commoditised: stuff is done to or for them a lot of the time. Many of my clients are resistant to the idea that they can do things for themselves.

I referred to anomie earlier; to me, this state of being not only includes a proclivity toward deviance, but also includes giving up. (Durkheim's work was initially on the power struggle and later about suicide.) If one is marginalised enough to be on the far edges of day-to-day life—a struggle even to make a cup of tea—what incentive is there to take any other responsibility on, especially one more onerous than making a cup of tea?

And, whilst it is not beyond the skills of the more experienced therapists amongst us to help people over this hurdle, there is a big question here as to whether solution focus is suitable for everyone. Some people just need a little comfort or advice, which are not usually the gift of the solution-focus specialist, but I bet you a cup of tea, some do it.

REFERENCES

Ajmal, Y., & Rees, I. (2001). *Solutions in schools.* London: BT Press.

Duncan, L., Ghul, R., & Mousley, S. (2008). *Creating positive futures: Solution focused recovery from mental distress.* London: BT Press.

Perry, R. (n.d.). Downloaded February 13, 2010, from http://ezinearticks. com/?Alienation-and-Anomie&id=433311

Rhodes, J., & Ajmal, Y. (1995). *Solution focused thinking in schools.* London: BT Press.

25

EXTREME LISTENING

Taught by People With Asperger's Syndrome

Vicky Bliss

I have one of the best jobs in the world. One reason I say this is because every time I meet with someone as a solution-focused therapist, I get to learn lots of things I didn't know before. In order to take full advantage of each learning opportunity, it is very important that my head is empty at the start of each session. Although this was a little scary at first—like working without a safety net, I have now gained the benefit from and grown quite accustomed to having an empty head.

The second reason I say I have one of the best jobs is because the people with whom I most often meet as a solution-focused therapist have Asperger's syndrome (AS).[1] By virtue of having neurological differences that affect the way they take in, store, retrieve, and use information, people with AS have a unique understanding of almost every aspect of the world around them. They frequently use words in a literal sense (so the phrase "pull your socks up" results in…well…reaching down and pulling their socks up) and their beautifully unique reasoning leads to unexpected associations and conclusions (so "worries" are not necessarily something to get rid of because without worrying, the person might get into danger).

You see? An ordinary, run-of-the-mill therapist might well come unstuck if he or she already had a head full of ideas about what the client needs to do in order to "get better." An ordinary, run-of-the-mill therapist simply won't do for people who have Asperger's syndrome.

The kind of therapist that works best with people who have their own unique views of what they want in the future (which is pretty much everyone, but I restrict my writing here to people with AS) is precisely one whose only two aims for a therapy session are to learn what it is the clients want and how they will know when they are moving in the right direction. The rest of the therapist's mental space is thus empty and ready to receive new information from the client.

However, all is not as it seems because clients rarely state exactly what their aims are and even less rarely come to therapy prepared to state the small steps that will tell them they are moving purposefully in the right direction. Many people with AS are sent to therapy and do not actually know what will constitute successful work by the standards of the person who sent them. Many people with AS do not know what is offered within therapy. Still more people with AS struggle to imagine a future that might be different from the present circumstances. Quite a few people with AS say they are not used to being asked what their aims are or to being asked for signs of success along the way. Still other people with AS struggle to find the right words to express their preferred futures and their small steps of success. They may use words that are grammatically correct and sound appropriate without sharing a common understanding with the therapist about what these words mean.

Some people with AS believe the therapist is the person who will change things for them, rather than signing up to do anything different themselves. A few people with AS have no changes at all in mind, but are too polite to terminate the sessions or perhaps enjoy the company of the therapist too much to discharge themselves. A lot of people with AS assume the therapist already knows everything about them, along with what they need to do to "get better," and become almost unhinged at the idea that the therapist is relying on them to provide the direction and the small steps! These people have been told, in error of course, that the therapist is the expert who will know what to do.

"Oh dear," is a frequent response of mine, followed by a version of

> Listen, you and I are pretty smart people. [pause] Do you think that if you and I work really well together we can work out what a good future for you might look like? [pause] What I mean by "work together" is that I'll ask a lot of questions, you do your best to answer them, and then I'll do my best to understand. Is that worth a go?

If the person with AS says, "No," then most likely we will not continue with a therapeutic relationship, though I do have other questions up my sleeve for just such mental emergencies. If the person is willing to have a go, then my main intervention becomes what my colleague in health psychology, Dominic Bray, has termed "extreme listening" (personal communication, December 14, 2008). Extreme listening involves the following considerations before engaging in solution-focused therapy:

1. Abandoning preconceived values and notions about the client and the outcomes of therapy.
2. Having a true belief that each client knows what he or she wants to do differently, will know when he or she is moving in the right direction, and has at least some of the skills needed to achieve the desired change. If you doubt these, resign.

And one main consideration once engaged in therapy:

3. Listen like a person possessed.

DESCRIPTION OF THE INTERVENTION

Preconceived Values

Extreme listening means going into a session with no idea about what needs to be discussed or what the outcome of the session ought to be in order to be helpful to the client. People with Asperger's syndrome are often sent to therapy because they behave in ways that are difficult for other people to manage. For example, they may spend money that they do not have and run up bills for which their family members feel responsible. Some people with AS truly do not understand the idea of getting something now and paying for it later; thus, when offered something—as they see it—for free, they are keen to take advantage of this offer and they bring home things they often do not need or want. Family members do not understand how their son or brother can understand astrophysics but not understand the concept of debt and heated arguments result. The general practitioner (GP) may refer this man with AS to therapy for anger management or something similar.

Extreme listening will be required in order to hear what the man's aims for therapy might be, and if a therapist goes into the session with a belief that the goal will be to get the person to stop spending so much money or to manage his anger better, the therapist will not be able to listen well enough. In my all-too-frequent experience of this situation, the client's aim is likely to be something to do with getting the family off his back rather than changing his own behaviour. Without extreme listening, it will be easy for the therapist and client to trot off in two nonintersecting directions for therapy.

Extreme listening, particularly when working with "labelled" individuals who we easily assume have characteristics in common, means hearing things that may not fit with preconceived ideas of how "these people" think, feel, or behave. For example, people with Asperger's syndrome are not supposed to be able to read nonverbal language very well. A solution-focused therapist who is good at extreme listening will be quick to notice exceptions to this when the client correctly reads the nonverbal language of the therapist. The resourceful solution-focused therapist will be able to talk with the client about the detail of how that exception occurred, even though popular beliefs say that people with AS are not supposed to have that skill. Thus, an extreme listener will not be fooled into thinking that what "ought" to be the case for a group of people is the reality for any individual within that group. In fact, a good extreme listener will have no idea as to what "ought" to be the case in the first place.

True Belief in the Client

The second consideration in preparation for extreme listening is that the therapist really believes that the person they are about to meet knows what they want to change and what they want to keep in their lives. Furthermore, the therapist must really believe that the client will recognise when they are moving in the right direction and will possess some of the skills required to start achieving their preferred future.

When clients belong to minority groups, such as people with Asperger's syndrome, it can be challenging to therapists to believe that these people—with their different ways of thinking, their abandonment of social conventions, their nonemotional processing of information, their high levels of academic intelligence combined with their low level of social skill, and their sometimes confusing presentation—actually do know what is best for themselves. If therapists do not get straight in their minds that people know what is in their own best interest, they will be unable to practice extreme listening. If such doubts surface, therapists need to lie down in a darkened room until their afflictions pass. If they do not pass, they need to resign from solution-focused work.

The critical nature of this fundamental belief in people with Asperger's syndrome can be illustrated by one young man who lives with and has frequent loud arguments with his mother. His mother wants him to stop being so aggressive with her, to stop spending money they do not have, and to follow through with things he says he is going to do, like joining a gym. He is talked about by people who know him as a man of few skills, having spent his education in a special school and lived with his mother for all of his life. He refuses to see me without his mother present, defers to his mother in response to all my questions, and does give the impression of passivity. It is hard to imagine him roused to an aggressive pitch.

A team of professionals are also involved, including a psychiatrist, social worker, occupational therapist, and support workers who take him on day trips without his mother. Most people involved with him, including his mum and granny, know what he needs. He needs a job, medication, a diagnosis, increased self-esteem, a firm hand, boundaries, consequences for his behaviour, and more structure, along with a list of other similar things.

It was hard to quieten these voices when I first met with this young man. It was hard to listen to his silence, listen to his expressions and other nonverbal language, and listen to what his mother was saying at the same time. His expression seemed more interested when his mother was talking about why she had hope that things could be better in the future than it was when she was listing his faults. His expression when his mother said all the things that he had to change was not positive or interested. Toward the end of our time, I gave rather more of a soliloquy than I am used to giving, though in the absence of verbal participation from him, it seemed like an acceptable risk to take.

I wondered aloud how it came to be that such a handsome, fit, talented, funny, bright young man (all things his mother had noted) was living in a situation where he was upset so much of the time. I wondered where he learned to sit so quietly and politely whilst his mother said both good and not so good things about him. I wondered if the time with me had been well spent and how I would get to know what he wanted for the future that might be different from what his mother wanted for him. And I wondered how he would know when it was a good idea to talk to me, maybe without his mother present.

If I did not believe that this young man knew what he wanted, knew how to start getting what he wanted, and had some of the skills to attain what he wanted, I would very likely have come away with a plan to help him manage money and/or manage his anger.

Listen Like a Person Possessed

Extreme listening is characterised by listening like a demon, as though one's therapeutic life depends upon coming to a joint understanding about what the client wants. It means listening twice as much as talking, with ears befitting the largest elephant. It means checking out every bit of data with the client. It means going for the detail of what the client means. It means asking lots of questions and listening to each answer. It involves developing an obsessive, demented need to understand exactly what it is the client means when he or she says "happy" or "relaxed" or "worry" or any other of the thousands of possible words he or she might use. Extreme listening means never assuming one understands.

For example, people with AS who come for therapy seem often to talk about being "worried." They may say they worry about being able to cope with unexpected situations, about falling ill, or about being lonely. A typical listener could easily run into difficulty by assuming that the person wishes to worry less or to stop worrying altogether. An extreme listener, however, would know to listen very carefully to the client's answers about how the worrying is helpful, about the place of worry in their preferred future, and about how they will know when they are worrying just the right amount. A good extreme listener takes nothing for granted.

Extreme listening is also characterised by hearing things that are *not* said, as in the example of the young AS man who lived with his mother. People with AS are sometimes slow to engage in a conversation, so the extreme listener may only have nonverbal language with which to develop more questions about the person's preferred future.

An extreme listener, like an extreme sports person, will listen even when the conversation goes *off piste*. The extreme listener will be brave enough to follow the conversation of the client, even when that discussion goes far away from the problem, where conventional therapists might fear to go! As mentioned earlier, people with AS are frequently referred for therapy by a third person for things like anxiety or depression or poor social skills. Whilst recognising it is important to pay attention to the goals of the person making the referral, the extreme listener will not hesitate to go with the client into areas that are not obviously related to anxiety, depression, or poor social skills. The listener might follow the client into areas of physics, maths, or music, or talk about other interests of the client. For some, spending an hour talking about the interests of a client might not seem like good therapy; however, for the extreme listener, much useful information will be gained about what the person would like more of and less of in the preferred future by having just such a positive conversation.

A really good extreme listener, again like a good extreme sports person, practices and practices and practices and sometimes gets a headache.

HOW DOES IT FEEL TO BE REALLY LISTENED TO?

People with AS who come for therapy say they are not used to being listened to; isn't that sad? I didn't know that until a group of people with AS told me so. A routine part of my practice is to ask each individual what has been helpful about the solution-focused work, and a surprising number of responses are about being really listened to. One individual with AS put this quite well when he said that other professionals only half-listened, then they filled in the blanks with what *they thought* was wrong, whereas he felt I listened to him 100%. He said he knew I was listening because I used his words in my responses and because I asked a lot of questions until he was sure I understood what he was meaning. He—and others have agreed—liked it when I could tell him what he meant and it matched with what he intended to mean.

Within sessions, people who are not used to being *really* listened to appear surprised by the nature or perhaps the intensity of extreme listening by the therapist. Dialogue consists mainly of questions from the therapist, and a person with AS may want a bit of time to practice in the new role as teacher. A sensible answer to many solution-focused questions is, "I dunno," often followed by a silent "?" from me.

Another possible response to extreme listening by a person with AS might be anxiety. People frequently come to therapy with the expectation that the therapist will know (a) what is wrong and (b) how to fix what is wrong. An enthusiastic, extreme listener may be a worrying development to some clients. "I don't know—you're the expert" is not an uncommon response to my questions.

Good extreme listeners will not be put off by these nondescript answers because of their adherence to the belief that people know what they want and that they will be able to recognise steps in the right direction. Questions to elicit information about preferred futures and next steps can be asked in many ways. One question that doesn't elicit a meaty answer can be followed by another question that might work better.

With practice, clients appear to become relieved that there is no "right" answer and no question to which they "ought" to know the answer. This "trial and triumph" type of question and answer relationship frequently leads then to a more relaxed joint type of working where both client and therapist sit on the same side of the table and work out together how to gather the information needed to move forward. The expertise of the extreme listener leads then to a "let's find out together" kind of productive relationship.

CONCLUSION AND CONTRAINDICATIONS

People with AS are great at teaching therapists how to succeed at extreme listening. Their unique ways of processing information require a therapist who is good at extreme listening—one who has faith that having AS does not exclude an individual from knowing what he or she wants and how to get it.

Extreme listening is not listed as a technique within solution-focused brief therapy; however, it is an essential aspect of this kind of therapeutic work. Without exceptional listening skills, the therapist will have no framework, structure, or direction to the therapy and neither the client nor the therapist will know when a successful end has been reached. Careful extreme listening will be important with any client from any background, of course, though a therapist can get especially good practice at this skill when working with someone from a different culture using a different set of values from that of the therapist.

Extreme listening can lead to overly enthusiastic questioning as the therapist casts about for a direction in therapy. There may be occasions when this creates anxiety for the client. A therapist who adheres rigidly to the core beliefs of solution-focused work, however, will be able to trust that, in time, a good combination of questions and answers will result in both therapist and client travelling together down the road to the client's preferred future.

NOTE

1. Asperger's syndrome—think "geek" or "Spock"—refers to people who are usually very intelligent in certain areas such as mathematics, physics, engineering, art, or any number of other areas and, at the same time, struggle to talk about everyday things like the weather. They usually do not grasp the importance of emotions and miss nonverbal language cues, thus appearing awkward in social situations.

26

BIG BROTHER

Lyndsey Taylor

At the time of my undertaking a piece of work, *Big Brother* was on the television. This is a UK reality TV show often calls participants into the "diary room" to speak to Big Brother about their thoughts and feelings.

Judith Milner and I were the therapists. The children we were working with enjoyed *Big Brother,* so we wondered how to use this to our advantage to engage them and make things more interesting, particularly for the older children. We were well aware that in order to keep the children's enthusiasm for this piece of work, we needed to be creative in our thinking.

During one session with the family, whilst playing "Respect Bingo" (a solution-focused tool for working with families), two middle children, ages 11 and 7, had a falling-out that resulted in the 7-year-old's crying and storming off from the room. Judith said to the room in a loud voice, "This is Big Brother. Would Terrence (age 11) and Amanda (age 7) please come to the diary room?" At this, Terrence picked a corner of the living room. He pretended to open a door, walk in, and proceed to sit down on the floor. He said, "Good afternoon, Big Brother" as the rest of the children and his parents sat and watched in silence. At this point, Amanda was not willing to join in the fun, so the conversation continued with Terrence alone.

Big Brother (Judith) said, "There's been lots of arguing and shouting in the game today. What do you think you could have done to help Amanda calm down?" Terrence replied, "I think she's tired and needs an early night." Big Brother then asked if Amanda was likely to get that today and Terrence replied, "She can go to bed early tonight." Big Brother asked what else Terrence could do to help Amanda right now. He replied, "I could go talk to her and ask her to come back into the room so we can hear if we've all done well today." With this, he went off to speak to his sister. They returned to the room 2 minutes later, calm and ready to hear how well they had done. Terrence received that day's reward and everyone, including Amanda, was in agreement with this!

Throughout the following weeks, Terrence adapted the Big Brother approach to sorting out problems or diffusing situations by holding his nose to make a remote sounding voice and calling people to the "customer information desk." In essence, this was a similar approach that diffused tantrums and afforded all of the family to have their voices heard. It was more effective than the Big Brother idea because the person with the (pretend) microphone at the customer information desk not only mediated tantrums but also made decisions when there was no agreement.

For example, when three family members claimed a reward, the customer information desk decreed that the reward be shared. At the same time, this enabled the other children and parents to listen to who was having the tantrum and decide on ways to remedy the problem. Through discussions with the parents, they were able to understand how acknowledging the children's feelings was extremely important in order that they felt listened to and that their problems were validated. However, by using this approach, the problem would not be dwelled upon and they would be assisting their children in working toward a solution.

CONCLUSION

The most pleasing aspect of working with this family was the way they responded creatively to fun ways of handling upset and arguments, especially the ideas of the customer information desk. This worked well because it was the family's own solution. Should you have experience of large chaotic families coming up with creative solutions, I would love to hear about them.

27

ENGAGING THE IMAGINATION

Rob Black

The future is unwritten.

—Joe Strummer

The underlying theme of the solution-focused model is associated with the future co-construction between the therapist and the client of a picture of what life might look like if the problem were solved or being dealt with more effectively. The miracle question (de Shazer, 1988) is widely recognised as a staple in the solution-focused practitioner's repertoire.

I have asked many miracle questions that have in turn led to countless descriptions of many alternative preferred futures. As a solution-focused practitioner, there have been occasions when my clients/young people have struggled when asked the miracle question. This has been a constant challenge and dilemma for me as a worker; what do you do in such situations? My suggestion is that you bring the boundaries of the conversation into the vision of the young person. It is my aim within this chapter to share with you some of my own experiences and ideas in co-constructing a preferred future.

I have worked with young people for over 20 years and have always found that showing a genuine interest in their worldview promotes conversations that are rich in interests, abilities, hobbies, and passions. Utilising these aspects of the young person's own personal makeup can sometimes increase the possibility of developing a pathway to his or her own perceived preferred future. The key is to establish a dialogue that gives the client the opportunity to give a description of life without the problem/presenting issue in as much detail as possible through a lens that fits the client's worldview.

Finally, a solution-focused coach will assume that the words that ultimately make a difference are the words a client hears himself or herself say. The coach's job is to ask the questions that release these words. Put another way, clients are seen as the expert in their own lives even though they will not always be aware of their expertise. The skill of the solution-focused coach is to follow each of the client's answers with a new but related question until the client hears the words that describe their knowledge (Iveson & George, 2009).

In the early part of 2007, the UK supermarket chain Tesco undertook a survey of young people throughout the UK in which they asked what the young people considered to be their favourite possessions. Interestingly, at the top of the lists came gadgets: gadgets that complete homework, change parent's behaviours, make a continuous supply of fast food, make you more attractive, or transport you through time.

So what, you may ask, is the relevance of this to solution-focused practice?

Case Study: The Wishing Machine

Clients Ben and Paul were referred to Social Services due to their constant fighting and arguing and generally not having the best of relationships. Both boys had been diagnosed with attention deficit disorder; their mother believed this added to their disruptive behaviour. The family agreed that a successful outcome for the work would be for them to "get on better" and "fight less." At the initial session, both boys found it very hard to concentrate. They would often get up, walk around the room, and pay little attention to what they perceived as my boring questions. These boys just wanted to have fun!!

The worker's task. As Iveson et al. (2003) suggests, the solution-focused worker/ practitioner's task is based on a clear framework:

- Find out what the person is hoping to achieve from the meeting or the work together.
- Find out what the small, mundane, and everyday details of the person's life would be like if these hopes were realised.
- Find out what the person is already doing or has done in the past that might contribute to these hopes being realised.

The challenge for me seemed clear: Could I engage these boys in a conversation to highlight a goal for our work? Elicit the signs and signals of improvement if their goal/ hope was achieved via their preferred future? And, finally, try to discover what they were already doing that was helpful?

The mother in this case was very clear about her best hopes for our meetings— that is, for her boys to have a better relationship. The boys were less clear initially but did acknowledge their mother's wishes. The boys were quite playful, although totally oblivious to my questions. It appeared that their main sense of enjoyment consisted of messing around with the acetate paper they had somehow managed to acquire from the cupboard and their main focus of dialogue revolved around the gadgets they liked at home and what they liked doing with them. Given that this was the only aspect of the conversation they showed any interest in, it seemed logical to me to use it as a way of getting some dialogue going.

Worker: So, I am curious; suppose there was a machine or gadget that could sort this stuff out between you—you know, the fighting and the arguing—would that be useful?

Ben and Paul (in unison): Yeah, probably it would be something.

Worker: OK, you say that would be useful. Do you think between now and next time we meet you could give this idea some thought and design or draw such a machine or gadget that would help you to get along as brothers?

Ben and Paul: That sounds like fun! Can we use this paper? [they hold up the acetate]

Worker: I don't see why not. OK, I will see you both next time.

At the family's request a session was booked for the following week.

Next session. Ben and Paul returned and were equally as energetic and roamed freely around the room. I had optimistically set up the overhead projector to display their work; both boys were eager to project their image onto the wall (see Figure 27.1)

Worker: Wow, that's quite an impressive looking thing! What's it called?

Ben: We call it the wishing machine.

Worker: The wishing machine…what's it made out of?

Ben: Well, it's made out of steel, metal, bits of broken cars, stuff like that, and the handle is made of silver and bronze.

Worker: How big is it?

Ben: Pretty big, say about 6 feet tall and say 6 feet wide.

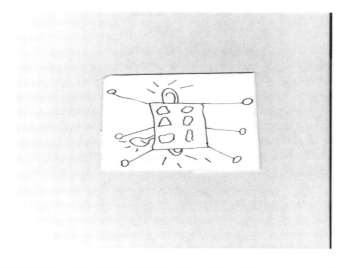

Figure 27.1 The wishing machine.

Worker: How do you get this thing to do its stuff?

Ben: You pull the handle and this big cloud of smoke comes out and lands on Paul and me and makes us friendly.

Worker: How do people know the wishing machine has worked?

Ben: Pardon?

Worker: I am just interested: When the smoke clears, how would, let's say, your mum know that the wishing machine had done its job?

Ben: Like I said, me and Paul would be doing friendly stuff.

Worker: Friendly stuff? What kind of friendly stuff would she see you doing?

Ben: Well, me and Paul not fighting!

Worker: I see: not fighting! So what would you be doing instead?

Ben: Playing games, getting on.

Worker: What kinds of games would you be playing?

Ben: Hide and seek, tag, Monopoly Junior.

Worker: I see. And what difference would this make to your mum?

Paul: She would be pleased with us.

Worker: And how would you know that she was pleased?

Ben: Erm…well, she would probably smile, wouldn't you, Mum?

Mum: Yeah. I would be really surprised!!

Worker: So it would be a real surprise, Mum?

Mum: A big surprise!

Worker: And who else might notice these changes, Mum?

Fantasy to reality. And so the description of the boy's preferred future in terms of their relationship begins. What initially began as a daunting task for me as worker had, by changing the medium, allowed the boys to describe in concrete behavioural terms the small indicators and signs of a way forward and what other people would notice.

Of course, the constructing of machine gadgets is steeped in complete fantasy. However, making its purpose specific—that is, it resolves the presenting issue/problem—allows the outcome of the conversation to be set in reality.

Case Study: The Storyboard Miracle

One 9-year-old girl I worked with did not want to speak during the first session and responded by nodding and shaking her head. She stated that she wanted to communicate her answers to my questions by drawing and writing them on the flip chart in the room because she found it difficult initially to verbalise her answers. As Selekman (1997) stated, "Young children have a tendency to express themselves through nonverbal communication such as play and art activities."

Because the young person in this particular case loved drawing, it seemed an obvious step to tap into this resource in order to help in the development of our work together:

Worker: Can I ask you a crazy question?

Young person: [nods her head]

Worker: I would like you to think about this strange and unusual question, as it requires a lot of thought and imagination on your part. Let's suppose that, when you leave here today, go home, and go to bed, while you are sleeping a miracle happens and the problems that brought you here today disappeared. But you did not know this miracle had taken place because you were asleep. Tomorrow

Figure 27.2 Storyboard miracle.

morning when you wake up, what would be the first thing/sign that would tell you a miracle has happened? Could you draw what this day might look like after the miracle?

Figure 27.2 is an example of a storyboard miracle. The drawing can act as the catalyst/template, hopefully, to begin a future-oriented conversation.

Worker: That's a fantastic picture! So much detail and it seems like there's a lot going on.
Young person: [smiles and says, "Yes," much to the worker's and Mum's amazement]
Worker: So what's happening in the first section?
Young person: That's me getting out of bed. I am the first person up!
Worker: Ok, you're the first person up. What difference does that make?
Young person: Well, my mum would not be shouting at me to get out of bed.
Worker: OK. So mum would not be shouting at you; what would she be doing instead?
Young person: She would be pleased with me as she could get on with other things.
Worker: And what difference would that make?
Young person: Well when my mum is happy with me she acts calmer; we have more fun then, you know, like get on better.
Worker: Sounds like that's helpful for you both.

So the conversation is developed around the presented images and the possibility of a way forward starts to emerge.

Collage of Signs and Signals

This is a simple exercise that I have found helps young people to focus on the qualities and changes that they or other people might notice if the presenting issue were resolved. Items needed include a flip chart pad, flip chart stand, pens, magazines, and glue. Ask the young person to draw an outline of himself or herself on the flip chart, leaving ample space to be filled. As the worker, I then pose the question, "OK, let's say tomorrow when you wake up, the problem that brought you here today is resolved. What changes would people notice about you that would tell them that you were starting to move forward?"

The young person or client will then fill in the body space with words and actions that would be noticeable if the issue were resolved (see Figure 27.3). Once those signs

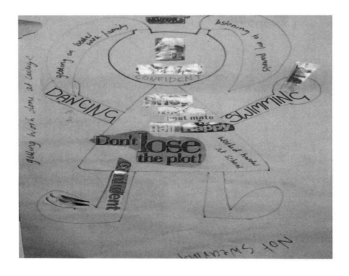

Figure 27.3 Collage of signs and signals.

have been identified, the worker will then be curious about any ideas the client may have about putting some of the actions highlighted into place, leading on to find out what difference that may make to his or her life.

CONCLUSION

These are just three examples that illustrate how a preferred future question can be creatively constructed. As a solution-focused practitioner over the years, I have tapped into anything from the world of *Star Wars* to the great *SpongeBob SquarePants*; the possibilities are indeed endless. Connecting with the young person's or child's given choice of communication, passion, interest, or personal strengths provides the worker with extra pathways to the preferred future scenario, incorporating the young person's own vision of life without the problem and a possible way forward. Young people or children have the ability to express their desired preferred futures clearly when given the opportunity; the solution-focused practitioner's task is to find the platform that supports their worldviews and gives them windows with which to look through and describe life without the shackles of the presenting issue.

REFERENCES

de Shazer, S. (1988). *Clues: Investigating solutions in brief therapy.* New York: Norton.

Iveson, C., & George, E. (2009). High-impact coaching. Unpublished paper.

Iveson, C., Ratner, H., & George, E. (2003). Handout from "Staying Brief with Children and Families," workshop presented at the BRIEF Therapy Center, March 27–28, London.

Selekman, M. D. (1997). *Solution focused therapy with children: Harnessing family strengths for systemic change.* New York: Guilford.

28

BREAKING DOWN BARRIERS

Paul Avard

The young people I work with in school and elsewhere are almost all mandated by a concerned teacher, pastoral manager, occasionally a parent, sometimes a friend, perhaps a youth or social worker, or other statutory agency: Seldom do they voluntarily want to come talk with me. Yet, of the hundreds and hundreds of young people with whom I've worked over the past several years, I've only ever had two flatly refuse to be in the room with me. I'm not a better therapist or counsellor than others, but I really do believe that persistent, prolonged exposure to children, young people from 11 to 16 years of age, has taught me to be child-like, to like, to respect, and to be mindful of and with them.

I have worked with young people in secure adolescent settings; in both on- and off-campus special-ed units; and in special residential, adolescent social care centres. Classrooms, youth centres, and day centres all figure in there somehow. I've worked with murderers (14 years of age), rapists (12, 13, and 14 years of age), prostitutes (male and female: youngest, 11 years of age), addicts, burglars, the homeless, the aimless, the rootless, the let-down: unloved, abused, unwanted, and tired. They've been Black, White, Asian, and any admix thereof; working class (blue-collar); white middle class; gang members; loners; isolates. Full of hate, full of hope, full of despair, full of love. Tearful, raging, submissive, seditious, rebellious, visionary, honest…

What can I do? The best I can. How can I hook them in, these unreachable kids? It's OK to call them that. I always apologise when

127

I forget and do it, and, to a person, they always laugh or at least smile, quizzical and wondering why this adult would bother to say sorry. Then they say, "It's OK; we know what you mean."

For some, the initial interview can be a real trial. To get beyond the hostile silence that young people who have been "volunteered" for support can give off, I look for ways to engage them and, whilst silence can be as fruitful as "noise," this isn't always so in the first meeting. So it occurred to me to use as natural an "in" as possible: I have a pad to jot down notes, so why not carry a second pad and some pencils, or felt-tipped colouring pens?

So, I usually have a pad of paper with a couple of pencils or pens available. Then, if they want to, the young person I'm working with can doodle; write swear words (curses) or a shopping list; draw a joint, cannabis leaf, or the Jamaican flag—whatever they want. We will destroy it at the end of the session or they can take it with them, whatever is fine—except if there's something harmful or a threat on the page (assuming they've shown me, in which case I explain that I have to take everyone's safety into account, so I might have to share what they've noted or drawn). I guess, for them, it's akin to some kind of doing something other than what we are doing—engagement whilst being disengaged—a kind of "I don't need you doing good by me" (yet) and, no, this is not some sort of person-centred therapy or storyboarding.

I can count on the fingers of one hand the number of times this has got in the way of what I'm being retained to do. The young people usually don't bother with the pad next time, but engage with me to whatever degree they choose. The pad and pencils are there if they want them.

I only comment on their doodle if they ask and then only to compliment them on their engagement and the quality of what they've done, which sometimes surprises them:

"I wasn't paying attention, sir."

"That's fine. It was great meeting you today. Will you come here next week?"

Apart from two, they come back, and keep coming back.

29

WORKING WITH CHAOTIC FAMILIES

Lyndsey Taylor

INTRODUCTION

This piece of work involved a social worker, independent solution-focused practitioner, and a family of nine that consisted of mum, dad, and seven children aged between 4 and 14. The work was undertaken by Lyndsey Taylor (children and families social worker) and Judith Milner (independent solution-focused practitioner).

TURN TAKING

One of the most difficult parts about working with a large, rowdy family is *turn taking*. Even when adults are involved, you find that everyone has something to say and they seem worried that if they don't say it immediately, they'll forget it! During our work with the family, we talked about how important it was for everyone to "have their say," but also devised simple ways to ensure everyone took their turns. These included simple methods such as starting with the youngest child and ending with the oldest person in the room, or using an alphabetical approach.

Surprisingly, the children appeared to appreciate this simple approach and found it beneficial. The adults in the room also had to abide by the rules and the children therefore felt their views were as important as their parents' and social workers' views. In addition, the children knew their places within the group and were well aware of when they would be able to have their say. This avoided confrontation and conflict and allowed for the children to have a sense of empowerment. These approaches also helped reduce chaos both in and out of therapy, and during later visits, the family was observed to be less chaotic and calmer.

When deciding on an alphabetical turn-taking sequence, it is important to check how this will work out in practice. It was suitable for this family because the middle child's name began with an A, followed by the youngest child (D), and Mum (E). The middle children in this family were often overlooked. This caused them a great deal of anxiety and they often felt ignored, which meant that they made themselves heard by throwing tantrums and storming off. Creating a fair approach to turn-taking not only made conversations more harmonious, but also ensured that everyone's views, wishes, and feelings were heard. The youngest child in this family was 18-months-old and one of the major interrupters! Her views were sought by asking which family member could speak for her best.[1] It also meant that the children speaking for the younger children had to consider their wishes and feelings more.

When an alphabetical or age sequence is not appropriate, other methods can be used, such as using a toy. The person holding the toy gets the opportunity not only to speak but also to choose who gets it next. This gives children the power to shut up noisy family members, discourages grabbing, and encourages cooperation.

RESPECT/RESPONSIBILITY BINGO

Playing *Respect Bingo* proved a productive way of holding solution-focused conversations with this family about the key behaviours that needed to be developed as part of a family safe-care plan that would include Dad. We started by asking the four older children and their parents to explain their understanding of the words *respect* and *responsibility*. After generating a good list of descriptions for each desired behaviour, we wrote them on separate cards. Each one also was written in squares of bingo sheets; each sheet had some the same and some that were different. We then paired everyone (including the practitioners) to play the bingo game.

Imagine a card with five rows and five columns making 25 boxes. Each column was headed "Caring for Self," "Working With Others," "Responsibility at Home," "Fairness in Play," and "Trustworthy Actions." In each box is a statement such as "do chores without being reminded," "wait your turn," "ask questions when you aren't sure," "keep your promises," or "be where you say you will be." Buttons were used for marking the squares.

We read statements from the set of cards we had made with the family's statements. People playing looked at their boxes to see if they had that statement. Whoever had the statement on their sheet had to explain *how* they had done that action and it had to be evidenced by other family members before a button could be placed on the square. For example, one of the statements read out during a session was "does the dishes." This was a highly contentious issue because the children claiming this square thought they had done this, but Mum disagreed and said, "Is this when I have begged?" Judith responded with, "Perhaps after one reminder?"

Instead of arguing with Mum, the children competed amongst themselves for the shortest number of reminders and this afforded Mum an opportunity to be more positive about their behaviour. They were also able to agree to a task for the week ahead for the children to do the dishes with a maximum of one reminder each. They all happily agreed.

Dad claimed "take turns talking" from his bingo card, but was immediately denied it by his eldest boy: "You can't have that one. You always interrupt." Dad tried to argue that grownups interrupt because they think they're more right than kids, but was still challenged to "be more right without interrupting." "Listening more" became Dad's homework task. I attempted to claim the statement "being on time," which resulted in gales of laughter. I also received a homework task that week.

During one session of Respect Bingo, we were talking about keeping a positive attitude (under the category of "Caring for Self"), and both the children and parents were giving examples of how they did this with an example from the week. During this discussion, the youngest boy, age 5, shouted at his father, "and stop hitting mummy," at which both I and Judith were somewhat taken aback. Solution-focused conversations aim to give vulnerable family members a say in what safety will look like[2] and this seemed to us to be a perfect example of how it works in practice.

After each session, we would set homework for each other. This would be measured every week by the participants, but facilitated by either me or Judith. The people who achieved their goals that week would subsequently receive a reward. The eldest child, aged 13, agreed to "do her chores" one week and another agreed to "pick up trash from the ground." I agreed to "be on time" and everyone said they would "share their toys."

Judith and I returned the following week to discuss how things had been. Some of us did well and received a reward, whilst others recognised they could do better. Their homework would then continue for the following week. Rewards were always a tangible item that meant the children could see instant benefits and, in this respect, they were a helpful tool. Rewards could be anything from a sticker (monkey stickers seemed to work the best!) to a bag of sweets or a CD. However, rewards had to be given based on everyone's view of how things had gone throughout the week.

This tool could evolve easily with collaboration from family members and they could therefore decide what statements to have in each box. Having the family decide what goes in the boxes seems to be a particularly solution-focused way of working.

NOTES

1. For more details of how to give very young or severely disabled family members a voice, see Iveson, C. (1990). *Whose life? Community care of older people and their families.* London: B T Press, pp. 81–83.
2. See, for example, Turnell, A., & Essex, S. (2006). *Working with "denied" child abuse: The resolutions approach.* Maidenhead, Berkshire: Open University Press.

30

PAPER, SCISSORS, STONE
An Interactive Family Scale

Paul Hackett

INTRODUCTION

Often, I have found that sessions where children are involved can flag after an examination of the preferred future. This is particularly the case in offering sessions after school, when children may be missing out on playing with friends or watching favourite TV shows. In my practice, scaling usually happens after preferred futures and in subsequent sessions after a detailing of what's been better. I thought of adapting the game of paper, scissors, and stone as a way of bringing some energy and difference into the room when engagement is just beginning to drift away.

GENESIS

As is often the case in my practice, this idea occurred to me at a moment when I was unsure what to do. I was working with a very excitable 12-year-old boy with a diagnosis on the autistic spectrum. He generally enjoyed our sessions, but would often want to ask lots and lots and lots of questions. Some of these questions were helpful, some silly, some nonsensical, and some displaying wonderful insight. The difficulty was in trying to create some space to ask questions of my own rather than providing answers. For some reason, I asked the boy if he could play paper, scissors, and stone and he replied that he was a champion at it.

We agreed that for a short period of time during the session, whoever won got to ask a question.

PAPER, SCISSORS, STONE: A VERY SHORT INTRODUCTION

The way I was taught to play the game was for two people to each hold a closed fist in front of them. A count of three is taken; usually each person moves his or her fist to the count, and on three both display their hands. Paper is represented by a flat hand, stone by the fist remaining closed, and scissors with two fingers spread as if they were scissors. The rules are simple: Each possibility has a chance of victory based on the opponent's choice. Thus:

Paper wraps stone.
Stone blunts scissors.
Scissors cut paper.

As I say, this is a very short introduction. The game is generally played with two people facing each other and has nuanced psychological elements: Each tries to "read" the other's play as if there is some essence to the choice. For some it is taken with utmost (un)seriousness: There is a society that runs tournaments that are an Internet search away!

FROM HERE TO SCALING

Often in my work, an idea stays with me until it morphs into something else. I had a fourth session working with a family of four: mum, dad, and a boy and a girl, ages 8 and 9. This was a cold winter night after school and the telltale signs of flagging appeared after around half an hour. The kids had had a long day at school and the parents had rushed from jobs to collect their kids to be at the session.

I was at the point of asking for everyone's number on the scale, to which I sensed I would get bored replies, when I was reminded of paper, scissors, and stone. I asked the family if they had ever played this game and they had. So I suggested a quick variation: Using both hands, they were to think that the scale ran from the digits on their hands. Thus, zero would be two closed hands and ten would be all ten fingers showing. Ten was where they had achieved what they hoped for as a result of these meetings and zero the opposite. I suggested that we go on three.

All four family members had two fists in front of them and they moved up and down to the "one, two, three!" They displayed numbers that ranged from seven to nine. This took a little time to do as it is quite difficult to display the numbers on your hands. However, it injected such enthusiasm and humour into the session that it was well worth the effort. Each family member looked at the others' numbers and, before I had a chance to ask anything, they were enquiring into each other's choices. At the end of the session, with everyone looking flushed with fun, we agreed that this would be our last session but that they would keep each other on track by doing the hand scaling at home together as a family.

ONCE YOU START…

The change in atmosphere that this playful family scale generated in that session was something I was determined to try in other sessions. In essence, I discovered that families where there is a sense of connection between the members will happily engage in this fun activity. In utilising this scale, I have found that as well as generating energy in flagging sessions, it creates a space where family members engage with each other. Oftentimes I have taken a backseat whilst the family talked with each other about the choices on the scale. Often children have come in and gone straight to the scale, particularly if a reason for referral was due to their behaviour. Children are wonderful in wanting their achievements acknowledged—a lesson we adults would be wise to relearn.

I have found that the scale can quickly be suggested as a task—something like:

> Get together once a week and someone count to three and see where you all are. If you have gone down, only talk about what you might do to bring it back up. If things have stayed the same, congratulate each other on not letting it slip and only ask about what good things would happen if you were one finger higher. If you have gone up, say congratulations to each other and talk about what will keep it going.

If I set this as a task, I often print off these instructions and give them to each family member.

CONCLUDING THOUGHTS

As I said, families where there appears to be a connection between the members often engage best in this scale, but the task can be set for a family who generally avoids interacting as long as you have assessed their motivations as high enough. Most of the families I have used the scale with had children between the ages of 4 and 12. It is unlikely that using the scale could do any harm. It may be that the scale does not work with a family for whatever reason and the therapist ends up with egg on her or his face, but to my mind, a therapist with egg on the face often looks funny to family members, imperceptibly drawing them together! I would love to hear people's experience of using the scale. It is a simple idea that families appear to enjoy and gain benefit from.

31

DIABETES EDUCATION AND SUPPORT GROUP
A Different Conversation

Tommie V. Boyd and Yulia Watters

The Centers for Disease Control and Prevention classified diabetes as the seventh leading cause of death in the United States in 2008 and the prevalence and rise in the number of patients with type 2 diabetes (non-insulin-dependent diabetes mellitus experienced or adult onset) continues to be alarming. This systemic disease requires a lot of careful management by the patient. Unfortunately, care practices show relatively low compliance with doctors' orders based on this complex disease.

Different interventions that family therapists can offer to clients and patients can help them establish a different relationship with the illness and, as a consequence, often avoid devastating complications brought on by the inability to control blood glucose levels. Self-help coping strategies are well noted. In one setting, the solution-focused model and ideas have shown to work well in a group developed at a university setting with family therapists. This approach incorporates a multidisciplinary approach (Davis & Biltz, 1998) to patient care.

While working in a university medical school and outpatient clinic, we were inspired to learn more about the needs of patients diagnosed with diabetes and their concerns. In collaboration with the university's Health Professionals Division and Department of Family Therapy, we developed a diabetes support group based on patient and physician input. These two units worked together to provide emotional support and diabetes education for patients and their families.

We offered an opportunity for the attendees to receive the latest information, learn from various health care experts about managing the disease, build supportive relationships with others living with this illness, and improve strategies for coping and living with diabetes. The group was provided as a community service and met biweekly. It was important to accommodate patients and group members in an easily accessible facility and during after-work hours to promote a more regular attendance. Following the research that demonstrated families' powerful influence on health (Campbell, 2003), patients were encouraged to attend the meetings with family members.

The group formation was based on patient referrals provided by the university's health care clinic physicians as well as community physicians. Facilitators mailed support group information to patients from the university's internal medicine and geriatric clinics and posted flyers at other health care facilities on campus. Flyers were also mailed to physicians within the community. Group attendance began with a core group that consisted of four individuals and one couple.

Since all patients were diagnosed with the same illness, a nonhierarchical, reciprocal relationship among members emerged. One member, who was quite ill and recently discharged from the hospital, found strength to support other group members, especially when the conversation was about the beginning of a new treatment (insulin therapy). This attendee, who had many complications due to diabetes and had undergone multiple hospitalizations prior to the group experience, found himself in a position of an educator rather than a victim. He even stated that he never thought his negative physical experiences would be so useful to others.

This supportive group environment was reinforced by the utilization of de Shazer and Berg's (1992) solution-focused brief therapy (SFBT) ideas that we, as the facilitators, embraced during interaction with the attendees. The therapeutic approach was inspired by the SFBT tenets that "help clients resolve present problems by building on their existing resources and previously applied effective solutions" (De Castro & Guterman, 2008, p. 93). We found its fundamental assumption that clients know what is best for them to be most humanistic and respectful. We focused on promoting the client to notice a small behavioral change that probably was already happening, yet remained hidden as the person was focused on the manifestation of the problem. This perspective helped adopt a position of attentive listener for solutions, manifestations of resilience, and proofs of strengths.

Facilitators opened the initial session with inquiring what topics attendees would like to discuss and in which format (i.e., group discussion and/or presentation delivered by a health care professional). In this way, the facilitators remained curious about what was important for each member in the group and were ready to follow the patients' lead without imposing predetermined agendas. Selected topics included stress and diabetes, diabetes and quality of life, diabetes and art work, diabetes and body well-being, diabetes and social support, and diabetes: your health care team. In addition, two presentations were offered following the request from the attendees: "medications for the treatment of diabetes mellitus" by a representative of the university pharmacy department and "diabetes eye health and macular disease service" by a physician from the university eye clinic.

These topics were further defined in behavioral implementations during the presentation. For example, the session on diabetes and body well-being included information that produced discussions on such themes as eye, foot, skin, and dental care; control of cholesterol; and attendees' capacity to take care of self.

Each session had a particular topic and facilitators remained attentive to the suggestions of the members and their unique needs and goals. If one of the participants had a particularly difficult week, the group would spend time acknowledging the difficulty and promoting member contributions related to their experiences while facing the same situation. By addressing how participants were able to handle a presented situation successfully, the group was able to support any particular member with possible solutions and also gain some measure of control over their illness.

Participants often discussed that their illness was, at times, overwhelming. To be able to acknowledge these types of feelings and thoughts, participants were able to draw from others and identify other options for their particular situations. Facilitators often had conversations around the patients' capacity to be mindful about their food intake. Exceptions—times when the problem did not occur—and past successes, and capacity to handle the situation were emphasized rather than underlining the patients' difficulty or failure to manage their diets.

As one group member discussed the need to learn how to better control her blood sugar, we asked about how others managed this when they were away from home. After others pointed out that carrying snacks had made a significant change, the member was able to talk about how she could do this during the group session: snack and talk. This emphasis on the attendee's positive management created a difference that, once revealed, was seen as doable. Members' successes and positive changes received encouraging, positive comments.

During group activities, facilitators utilized different questions to assist attendees in accessing their resources and putting them into use

(Metcalf, 1998); in particular, scaling and relationship questions were helpful. Scaling questions consisted of asking, "On the scale of 1 to 10 (10 being the maximum control), how much control do you feel over your maintaining your current weight and blood sugar levels?" or "On a scale of 1 to 10 (10 being the highest), how do you rate your stress level based on your current circumstances?" This particular questioning was helpful to the attendees, as it often produced a discussion about the current management and exchange of ideas; this also supported their ability to monitor the development of a particularly desired behavior.

Another SFBT task was asking relationship questions of who noticed the changes experienced by the attendees or what was helpful in the implementation of these changes. For instance, one of the group members, who described himself as being very lonely, became more aware of the support he was receiving in his church and by doing so, became more engaged with his church members and in this group setting. Other members were able to identify outside resources as well, such as supportive neighbors, loving relationships of their relatives, and inner resilience. As group members were able to gain new insight and notice their changes and differences, they began establishing new connections, meeting friends, and returning to former pleasurable activities. This led to members' discussing their need to meet less often.

Along with the interventions, the termination process of this group embraced the solution-focused philosophy based on the therapist's commitment to lead from one step behind the patient (Pichot & Dolan, 2003). The facilitators allowed the attendees to see the end of the group meetings "as a process rather than an event" (Patterson, Williams, Grauf-Graunds, & Chamow, 1998, p. 219). Collaboration and consultation among physicians and therapists proved beneficial as information was available among all support systems.

CONCLUSION

Solution-focused brief therapy ideas provided attendees with a new way of addressing their diabetes and medical illnesses that originally seemed to rule their life. Participants acknowledged the benefits of the group, such as the positive focus and a supportive environment. Even after admitting that it was difficult for many of them to attend the group due to the unpredictability of the illness and transportation issues, all members stated the group was well worth their time. Upon completion of this group format and referrals to other groups and individual therapists, several members remained in contact and exchanged information. It was important to provide the attendees with an opportunity not only to receive information, but also to develop their "inherent drive toward wellness" (Heisler, 2007, p. 216). The solution-focused brief therapy approach guided this group process in achieving its objectives.

REFERENCES

Campbell, T. L. (2003). The effectiveness of family interventions for physical disorders. *Journal of Marital and Family Therapy, 29*(2), 263–281.

Centers for Disease Control and Prevention. (2008). *National diabetes fact sheet: General information and national estimates on diabetes in the United States, 2007.* Atlanta, GA: U.S. Department of Health and Human Services, Centers for Disease Control and Prevention.

Davis, T. F., & Biltz, G. R. (1998). Forming a multidisciplinary team. In A. Blount (Ed.), *Integrated primary care: The future of medical and mental health collaboration* (pp. 228–246). New York: W. W. Norton & Co.

De Castro, S., & Guterman, J. T. (2008). Solution-focused therapy for families coping with suicide. *Journal of Marital and Family Therapy, 34*(1), 93–106.

de Shazer, S., & Berg, I. K. (1992). Doing therapy: A post-structural re-vision. *Journal of Marital and Family Therapy, 18*(1), 71–81.

Heisler, M. (2007). Overview of peer support models to improve self-management and clinical outcomes. *Diabetes Spectrum, 20*(4), 214–221.

Metcalf, L. (1998). *Solution focused group therapy: Ideas for groups in private practice, schools, agencies, and treatment programs.* New York: Free Press.

Patterson, J., Williams, L., Grauf-Grounds, C., & Chamow, L. (1998). *Essential skills in family therapy: From the first interview to termination.* New York: Guilford Press.

Pichot, T., & Dolan, Y. M. (2003). *Solution-focused brief therapy: Its effective use in agency settings.* New York: The Haworth Clinical Practice Press.

II
Training

32

HOW DO PEOPLE LEARN SFBT?

Tomasz Switek

Exceptions: find them and describe with detail; ask about ideas of what helped them to happen.

Exceptions and experience of others: get to their stories and draw out ideas of what helped them to happen.

Knowledge: all possible sources that we can find; suggestions about what is worth doing and what is not worth doing; going toward personal conclusions that may be useful.

Conception work: experiments; transferring experiences from one field to another.

Total improvisation: go ahead and try.

Videotaping and videoanalyzing: observe; look for the meanings; develop ideas about what helped.

Live trainings: just do it and let's observe and then analyze; what was going on and what helped?

33

GOAL-SETTING QUESTIONNAIRE

Brenda Zalter

1. Suppose a miracle happened one night, and all your education needs for work with (fill in the blank—for example, adolescents, organizations/teams) were met through this training module. What would you be doing differently in your work with (adolescents, organizations/teams, etc.)?
2. How would this be helpful for you?
3. What would your colleagues notice you doing differently?
4. What things would you continue to do because they work?
5. On a scale of 1 to 10, how helpful do you expect solution-focused applications to be in your work?

What else would be helpful?

34

THE TRAINING MIRACLE QUESTION

Brenda Zalter

The following miracle question was used with staff at a hospital to help with day-to-day team building, conflict management resolution, and strategic planning:

Suppose, when this workshop ends, you go home, complete your day and get ready for bed. When you go to sleep, you fall into a very deep sleep and have one of the best rests you have had in a very long time. When you are sleeping, a miracle happens. The miracle is that all the difficulties you face as a manager/educator/clinical nurse specialist at (name of hospital/organization) are gone! Just like that! There are no complaints. Everything is running exactly the way you would want. You do not know this miracle has happened as you are sleeping. When you wake up and return to work the next day, what is the very first thing you will notice to be different that will make you stop and think, "wait a minute, some kind of miracle must have happened while I was sleeping because…"?

- How will this make a difference in your day-to-day ability to support/mentor your staff?
- What will your colleagues notice?
- How will this make a difference for you?

- What will your staff notice that is different about you?
- How will the patients know a miracle has happened?
- How will the hospital be different?

35

STRENGTH IDENTIFICATION

Lorenn Walker

Groups of four to six people are each given a set of five photos from Google or another Internet search engine of "poverty" or "poor people." The groups are given 30 minutes to review the photos and to list all the strengths that they see in them. After 30 minutes, each small group shares its list of strengths.

36

SOLUTION-FOCUSED DOMINOES

Tomasz Switek

My work as a group therapist and trainer has brought many questions about creating useful contexts for cooperation during group work. Therapy is a very talkative job to do, and during workgroups (especially longer ones) with clients or trainees, it is easy to observe signs of being tired by sitting, listening, and talking. I was thinking about different ways to respond and manage such situations as a trainer. Of course, we can still ask people what and how they want to act. Sometimes, however, it is more useful to have some propositions about connecting conversation with other activities. The concept of creating solution-focused games came through such experience.

Solution-focused games are propositions of connecting solution-focused assumptions and conversations with other activities so that we achieve new contexts where people start to play and have fun. Conversation during the ongoing process of play is very often more spontaneous, full of life and energy, and much easier to perform for large numbers of our trainees and clients.

We connect the solution-focused approach with very different ideas of traditional and new games. In this chapter, I present a game based on the concept of dominoes.

SOLUTION-FOCUSED DOMINOES

The goal of this game is to support people in small groups of three or four to have a nice time with useful conversation. Participants play the standard domino game and follow some additional rules that create an opportunity to talk about themselves, share stories and experiences, and, on that basis, notice their strengths.

INTRODUCTION

The game of solution-focused dominoes requires some preparation in order to use it in practice. First of all, you ought to buy a few sets of dominoes. Pieces should be numbered from 1 to 28. Each number on the particular domino piece refers to a specific question on a list. One such list appears at the end of this chapter. The types of the questions on the list should be addressed to specific needs of the participants or you can create general questions that may be useful for most participants. You should also print questions in order to give them to the participants of the game.

Divide participants into groups of three or four. Give one set of dominoes and at least one set of printed questions to each group. Then introduce the rules.

BASIC RULES

1. Each person chooses four dominoes.
2. The numbers on each domino refer to a question number on the list.
3. Follow standard domino rules.
4. When you put down dominoes, you have to complete the task given on the list.
5. If you don't want to answer, you miss your turn and you exchange the domino for a new one.
6. If you don't have the right number of spots to put down your domino, you take an additional one from the pile.
7. When one person is answering, the rest of the team can ask additional questions.
8. During the conversation, you can give (and write) compliments on the basis of the answer to a particular question.

QUESTIONS FOR SOLUTION-FOCUSED DOMINOES

Example Questions for the Group: General Exceptions

Example: Conversation About the Past

1. Tell us about how you showed your strong will.
2. Tell us how you controlled yourself in a difficult situation.
3. Tell us how you kept your word.
4. Tell us how you handled (dealt with) your weakness well.
5. Tell us how you were able to conquer your fear/worries.
6. Tell us how you did something good for yourself.
7. Tell us how you did something good for somebody else.
8. Tell us how you had a good time/enjoyed yourself.
9. Tell us how you were happy with yourself.
10. Tell us how you were enthusiastic about something small.
11. Tell us how you were happy with somebody else/shared your happiness with somebody else.
12. Tell us how much you strove for something/tried to do or get something.
13. Tell us how you found at least a little meaning in life.
14. Tell us how you were able to take a risk.
15. Tell us how you managed to resist temptation.
16. Tell us how you chose something good.
17. Tell us how you chose to be honest with yourself in a difficult situation.
18. Tell us how you chose to be honest toward others.
19. Tell us how you helped somebody else.
20. Tell us how you "got up"/recovered after an accident.
21. Tell us how you were able to fight for something.
22. Tell us how you did something unexpected.
23. Tell us what and how you were able to change.
24. Tell us how you were somebody's friend.
25. Tell us how you went back to something important.
26. Tell us how you managed to do something important.
27. Tell us how you showed your humbleness/humility.
28. Tell us how you managed to get involved in something important.

I tried to be brief in describing the concept of dominoes and its rules. You can get all instructions in ready-to-print format or ask questions by writing to tomaszswitek@centrumpsr.eu.

37

QUOTABLE QUOTES

Brenda Zalter

I use quotes for a team-building exercise. Everyone receives the following list and picks out a favorite quote. Small groups then talk about favorites and why they are favored, which leads to a great discussion on the topic.

When you're through changing, you're through.

—Bruce Barton

Never doubt that a small group of thoughtful, committed people can change the world. Indeed it is the only thing that ever has.

—Margaret Mead

You can't make footprints in the sands of time if you're sitting on your butt. And who wants to make butt prints in the sands of time?

—Bob Moawad

One pound of learning requires 10 pounds of common sense to apply it.

—Persian proverb

Accept that some days you are the pigeon and some days the statue.

—Dilbert, American comic strip engineer

We must be the change we wish to see in the world.

—**Gandhi**

Life is a process of becoming, a combination of states we have to go through. Where people fail is that they wish to elect a state and remain in it. This is a kind of death.

—**Anaïs Nin**

How wonderful it is that nobody need wait a single moment before starting to improve the world.

—**Anne Frank**

They say that time changes things, but you actually have to change them yourself.

—**Andy Warhol**

The important thing is this: To be able at any moment to sacrifice what we are for what we could become.

—**Charles Dubois**

If you have always done it that way, it is probably wrong.

—**Charles Kettering**

While we flatter ourselves that things remain the same, they are changing under our very eyes from year to year, from day to day.

—**Charlotte Perkins Gilman**

It is impossible for a man to learn what he thinks he already knows.

—**Epictetus**

Some men see things as they are and say, "Why?" I dream of things that never were and say, "Why not?"

—**George Bernard Shaw**

Things do not change, we change.

—**Henry David Thoreau**

Change does not necessarily assure progress, but progress implacably requires change. Education is essential to change, for education creates both new wants and the ability to satisfy them.

—**Henry Steele Commager**

You cannot step twice into the same river, for other waters are continually flowing in.

—**Heraclitus**

Change is the law of life. And those who look only to the past or present are certain to miss the future.

—**John F. Kennedy**

Just because everything is different doesn't mean that everything has changed.

—**Irene Peter**

Everyone thinks of changing the world, but no one thinks of changing himself.

—**Leo Tolstoy**

The whole course of human history may depend on a change of heart in one solitary and even humble individual—for it is in the solitary mind and soul of the individual that the battle between good and evil is waged and ultimately won or lost.

—**M. Scott Peck**

It's not so much that we're afraid of change or so in love with the old ways, but it's that place in between that we fear...It's like being between trapezes. It's Linus when his blanket is in the dryer. There's nothing to hold on to.

—**Marilyn Ferguson**

The truth is that our finest moments are most likely to occur when we are feeling deeply uncomfortable, unhappy, or unfulfilled. For it is only in such moments, propelled by our discomfort, that we are likely to step out of our ruts and start searching for different ways or truer answers.

—**M. Scott Peck**

Education is the most powerful weapon which you can use to change the world.

—**Nelson Mandela**

38

SUPERVISION E-MAIL FROM THE FUTURE

Steve Freeman

This piece of work is based on Yvonne Dolan's (1998) "letter from the future" exercise modified for supervision trainees. Both exercises are useful in defining goals, expressing preferred futures, and keeping both parties on track in supervision. A "supervision e-mail from the future" is practice based and is the result of many conversations with clients and colleagues over the years.

Solution-focused supervision is far from new. O'Connell (2001) and Briggs and Miller (2005) are good places to look. The question is not, "Why do solution-focused supervision?" but rather, "Why *not* do solution-focused supervision?"

The word "supervision" does not rest well with everyone. Some people find that it detracts from the "nonexpert" approach integral to solution-focused practice. And yet supervision is the term used by many people involved in discussing their clinical and/or academic practice. Supervision is certainly the term of choice for the people who have been part of generating the ideas for this piece of work. In this case, "supervision" does not imply that either party is "super" or "visionary."

My approach to supervision, regardless of the area of practice or the person's own approach is solution focused. It is not, however, dogmatic. Occasional bits of personal narrative or even advice creep into the conversations. Supervision tends to be longer term than most clinical work. Although an average three and a half sessions to get someone a master's degree or through 5 years working in acute mental health settings sounds very attractive, it is unlikely to happen. The principles that "brief" does not mean "time limited" (Simon & Berg, 1999) and taking as long as it takes (Ziegler, 1998) applies to supervision as well as it does to therapy.

One of the (many) appeals of solution-focused working is the natural fit in so many areas of work and for so many people. Solution-focused brief therapy (SFBT) and its principles applied in other areas, often referred to as a solution-focused practice (SFP), form the bedrock of my work in academia, research, health, and social care and management.

The supervision relationship discussed here can be related to both clinical practice and academic work such as research and dissertation production. The same principles and practices also apply to coaching environments. In fact, pretty much any solution-focused conversation with an element of preplanning and arrangement can make use of the e-mail from the future, subject to the obvious limitations of technology and literacy. These conversations can be based on face-to-face meetings, telephone, and e-mail contact.

Having tried a number of forms of "contracting" at the beginning of supervision and met with limited success, I decided to do something different. Contracting had, I believe, been less successful when neither party really knew at the start of the supervisory relationship what would or could happen as we moved along through the project, practice, or course of study. People do not, however, begin these journeys with empty heads; everyone with whom I have worked has made the effort to get their place on a course of study or post in practice with a clear idea of what was involved. This mix of best hopes for the future and not knowing what will happen can be the source of either a whole lot of frustration and disappointment or fertile conversations, depending on how it is handled by both parties.

Trusting the SFBT model is generally seen as useful and even essential. This basic tenet should, I believe, be a regular part of both supervision and reflective practice. Nothing in this chapter will be rocket science. It may, however, prove useful for people on both sides of the supervision relationship.

With a need for some understanding and common ground on which to work in supervision, it seemed that Yvonne Dolan's idea of a letter from the future would be a good starting point for any new supervisory contract. This has proved true of both individuals and groups. An e-mail from the future that sets the scene for one-to-one supervision can be translated into a great small-group exercise at the start of working with a group or team.

The e-mail from the future is not the first step in supervision any more than a letter from the future would be the first step in therapy. After agreeing to terms, I have asked some, but not all, of the people I'm working with to send me an e-mail from the future. The e-mail is written by the person, who imagines that he or she has successfully completed a course of study, dissertation, or project. The exact form varies from conversation to conversation and is informed by the clues given by the supervisee. The e-mail may include ideas such as:

> Having completed your master's and arrived at the graduation, a student who is just starting out asks you what supervision is about. What do you say based on your experience? How would you tell me about this conversation in an e-mail?" and "Sitting at home, admiring your certificate with friends and colleagues, what will have been important in achieving this? Who will notice how well you've done? Could you send me an e-mail following the conversation and describe what happened?

For clinicians, the e-mail would be written from some other appropriate point in practice—for example:

> It would be great if you could send me an e-mail from a point in 6 months' time when you're looking back at the positive changes that have happened in your practice" or "Some people find that a good starting point for supervision is an e-mail at that point in the future when you're reflecting on your career and some of the high points." More specifically, "Could you send me an e-mail from a year's time in which you highlight how supervision has been useful in your practice?

An example from a recent e-mail to a potential supervisee follows:

> No problem with supervision. Let me know which dates suit. I'm away for a couple of weeks in August but have a few gaps before then. Possibly best to give me a ring. As a starter, could you send me an 'e-mail from the future'? Pick a point in time 6–24 months from now and send an e-mail letting me know in what ways supervision has been useful and what the key factors were from your part and mine.

Groups producing e-mails from the future report negotiating and co-constructing their views of the e-mails' contents. They also report noticing how much they have in common in their aspirations for the group. People attending groups have reported that the thought and work involved in producing the e-mail before the group meeting can lead to presession change. As with all group work, more sets of best hopes are better than one. One exercise for a staff group seeking supervision was

> Suppose that our work together is successful. The team decides to let me know how much things have improved in the team. How about creating an e-mail from the future in which you describe what you're doing differently and how supervision helped?

Another exercise from a team seeking short-term support with changes in their work was

> So, let's imagine that our work with the team is successful. How about creating an e-mail together from a point in the future where you know it's OK? Tell me when this is, what is happening, and how our work together was useful.

My observation and feedback from graduates (they *all* graduate, of course!) and practitioners are incredibly congruent with the SFBT model and the use of the letter from the future in clinical practice. Having sent the e-mail, supervisees may or may not choose to discuss it early on in the supervisory relationship. On the other hand, they may use the e-mail as a way to set their own concrete goals early on in the conversation.

The overwhelming response is that supervisees, regardless of how they have used the e-mail, have been surprised at how close their achievements have been to the original e-mail. They also note how—often without thinking about it—the "plan" has worked out.

For my part as supervisor, I refer to the e-mail at the end of the course or at a review point in practice supervision. The e-mail is also useful in my discussions with my supervisor and in reflective practice. When I am stuck or if I feel confused, the e-mail is a point of reference or landmark for the work.

Whether we like it or not, supervision is a power relationship. Any power relationship can lead to abuse, neglect, and avoiding or simply missing the best hopes of the client. Lynne Gabriel (2005) discusses the "boundary riding" of therapists who have multiple roles (e.g., administrator, supervisor) and the similarities in the power relationships in supervision and therapy. The e-mail from the future, delivered to my inbox, helps to balance power and expertise. We know that anything that is in writing can be very powerful. Having someone's preferred future in an e-mail is powerful for both parties, and supervisors must be careful not to abuse the power or hold the e-mail over the heads of supervisees. As someone quipped recently, "I wrote it; you got it. We have a deal."

REFERENCES

Briggs J. R., & Miller, G. (2005). Success enhancing supervision. In T. S. Nelson (Ed.), *Education and training in solution-focused brief therapy* (pp. 199–222). New York: Haworth.

Dolan, Y. (1998). *One small step.* Watsonville, CA: Papier-Mache.

Gabriel, L. (2005). *Speaking the unspeakable.* New York: Routledge.

O'Connell, B. (2001). *Solution-focused therapy.* London: Sage.

Simon, J., & Berg, I. (1999). Solution focused brief therapy with long term problems. *Directions in Rehabilitation Counselling,* lesson 10, *10,* 117–127.

Ziegler, P. (1998). Solution focused brief therapy for the not-so-brief clinician. *Journal of Collaborative Therapies,* 6(1), 22–25.

39

THE ARTFUL DIAGNOSTICIAN

Bruce Gorden

Following is a slightly outrageous process, spawned in different supervision groups, for learning how to function as a therapist in an atmosphere dominated by the medical model metaphor, which pimps (utilizes) the DSM for purposes of diagnosis and treatment planning. We asked ourselves how we could function as strangers in a strange land without becoming corrupted ourselves.

When one masters the structure of the diagnostic process and "DSM-IV-speak," client intake, history, and treatment plan become almost automatic. Theory of pathology offers the right hand of fellowship to theory of treatment, and pathology and theory become one, with little or no need for a client. To guard against this, we developed a way of learning the structure of the DSM diagnostic process by *undoing* it.

Let's take borderline personality disorder, for example. We were frightened by it at first, but slowly, we found ways to disrespect the construct by profaning its name. We first called it "boarder" line—a description of a boarder who really wanted nicer digs, but had grown accustomed to less. Perhaps, it could just be a bad habit. Perhaps it was a good habit in a bad land. So, with the diagnostic process, we were taught to find the pesky symptoms no matter where they lay and call them for what they are: tiny clods of ailments, pieces of pathology, which have not yet coalesced into a respectful diagnosis. They are then imputed as characteristics. So, what if we *un*did that and went through an *un*diagnostic process?

Insoo Kim Berg, in a conversation with Heather Fiske, said that we should find stories of hope regarding this diagnosis (BPD) and tell them to others (Fiske, 2008). So we thought we should interview for stories of hope within each of the diagnostic criteria for BPD that follow. So, sandwiched among the DSM symptom menu items are some questions we thought of to keep in mind during intake and history taking. As good solution-focused interviewers, we were looking for exceptions— times when the problem was not happening—and then eliciting juicy descriptions of those times.

1. *Frantic efforts to avoid real or imagined abandonment.* The interviewer listens for the last time when there were fewer or no frantic antics when being abandoned, real or imagined. Perhaps the interviewer could ask about relationships in which there was a healthy attachment, or where there was more attachment and less abandonment. Maybe there were relationships in which the person knew that less involvement was better. How did they know?

2. *A pattern of unstable and intense interpersonal relationships characterized by alternating between extremes of idealization and devaluation.* We thought of scaling questions because none of us could find a relationship in which we did not do some idealizing and devaluing. Then we could ask where on the scale they would like to be. On that scale, what relationships seemed to be more like what the client wanted? What made them that way? What else...oh, and, what else?

3. *Identity disturbance: markedly and persistently unstable self-image or sense of self.* "What relationships are you in that you feel most yourself? What is it about that relationship that allows you to be yourself? Who would be most surprised about that? What about you comes out the most? What about that do you like the most? What kinds of people bring out the best in you?"

4. *Impulsivity in at least two areas that are potentially self-damaging.* "What are the areas of your life when that would never happen? Where is it just a little bit less so? With whom would it be most likely to occur? With whom would it happen less often? What is available to you that helps it not happen? How do you manage to stand against it?"

5. *Recurrent suicidal behavior.* Since this is recurrent, we are interested in the times when it is not happening. "How is it that you manage to keep hold of reasons to live during those times?" Again, they have a lot of experience NOT doing it. We want to learn how that happens. We refer the reader and group

supervisor to Fiske's (2008) book, *Hope in Action*. She offers a wealth of material on this subject.

6. *Affective instability due to a marked reactivity of mood.* We mostly generated scaling questions here: "When the mood is most reactive, where is your affect most likely to be on the scale? Where would you like it to be? What do you need to do when things are at a 7? How about 5? What is the difference? How do you do that?"

7. *Chronic feelings of emptiness.* "What happens when that feeling is getting filled? Who are the people most likely to know you are feeling a little fuller? What things do you do that have an effect? When you are at an 8, is it OK to go down a little? Where (on the scale) do you spend most of your time? When do you know it's time to bring it up some? What do you do then?"

8. *Inappropriate, intense anger or difficulty controlling anger.* "Last time you got angry, how did you know when it was time to do something about it? What generally works to keep it in check?" It is always a good idea to use scaling questions regarding affect: "When do those feelings work well for you? How? Oh? How else?"

9. *Transient, stress-related paranoid ideation.* These are generally relational symptoms as well and are amendable to scaling questions. So, we generated lots of questions about with whom, where, when, and how. Exception questions generated a lot of small and wonderful opportunities for making differences that made a difference.

As budding family therapists, we realize that when we make a distinction (e.g., diagnosis), we are part of the system making the diagnosis and therefore making self-referential observations. We also realize that we are interviewing for a pathological diagnosis, and interviewing to UNdo that very diagnosis. This is much like a crisis interview in which we must assess well for lethality, and for hope!! This process has served us well. We are not pure or untainted from having to converse in DSM-IV-speak, but we feel less slimed upon. We have done this for many other diagnoses, such as major depression. We hope you get the idea.

REFERENCE

Fiske, H. (2008). *Hope in action: Solution-focused conversations about suicide.* New York: Haworth.

40

CIRCLE EXERCISE

Arnoud Huibers

This circle exercise can be used to introduce the heart of solution-focused therapy. Foreknowledge or experience with the approach is not required. For this reason, the circle exercise is appropriate at the beginning of a training or workshop. The group size can vary from eight to 50 participants, who work in pairs. The trainer gives clear instructions, monitors the time, and leads the discussion. The exercise lasts 45 minutes. It is our experience that the circle exercise is met with much enthusiasm.

PURPOSE OF THE EXERCISE

The participants experience the power of strength-based questions through action learning in a safe setting. The questions focus directly on gained successes and on important goals in the life of the participant. After the exercise, the experiences of the participants are placed in the conceptual framework of the solution-focused therapy model so that it is better understood.

INSTRUCTIONS

The trainer asks the group to form pairs. One of the pair is the client, and the other is the therapist or coach; they do not switch during the exercise. The coach interviews the client, who gives answers from his or her own experience so that he or she does not need to play the role of someone else. Doing it this way is most instructive. The circle exercise is divided into five stages. The trainer gives instructions at the beginning of every stage and monitors the time.

Stage 1. Drawing Circles (10 Minutes)

The coach interviews the client concerning successes of last year (A) and goals for the coming year (B, see Figure 40.1). The coach writes down key words in the inner circle, for example, "diploma gained" or "house redecorated" (A) or "tidying up study" or "improving communication with spouse" (B). The coach appreciates the answers and shows interest by asking more details concerning the successes and goals. These strength-based questions empower the client.

A. *Successes of last year.* The coach asks, "What did you accomplish last year that you are pleased about? It can concern small successes or big successes both in your work and in your private life. It can also concern a problem that you solved or a difficulty you overcame; that is also a success."
B. *Goals for the coming year.* The coach asks, "What would you like to achieve by the end of the coming year in your work or

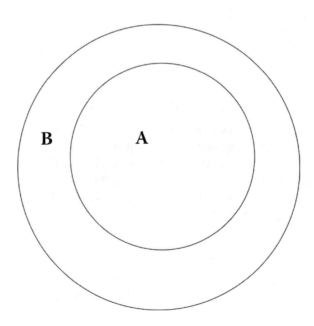

Figure 40.1 Past and future circles.

your private life? You can mention small, practical goals or bigger ones that need more time"

Stage 2. Feedback to Client (5 Minutes)

The coach summarizes what the client has said based on the key words that the coach has written down in the circles. The coach summarizes the client's achievements and important goals. Then the coach asks the client to make a selection and choose the two most important goals in his or her life at this moment.

Stage 3. Scaling Questions (15 minutes)

The coach assigns a scale of 0 to 10 for each of the two goals that the client has chosen. The coach asks, "What number would you give on a scale of 0 to 10 at this moment, with 10 meaning that you have reached your goal? What tells you that you are on a 4 or 5 or 6? How would you know that you have climbed one number on the scale? What will then be different?"

If the participants have never worked with scaling questions, the trainer needs to give clear instructions in advance. A demonstration is very welcome to show how scaling is applied, what a well-formed goal looks like, how questions about details are useful, and how one step forward can be stipulated (see Figure 40.2).

Stage 4. Feedback to Coach (5 Minutes)

Here, the clients give feedback to the coaches: What did they like about the exercise? Which questions that the coach asked were interesting and useful? What was pleasant about the style of the coach? The client also gives a number on a scale from 0 to 10 on how useful this exercise was to him or her. A 10 means that this exercise was very useful and 0 that the exercise wasn't useful at all.

Stage 5. Plenary Discussion (10 Minutes)

The plenary discussion is an important part of the circle exercise. The trainer asks about the experiences of the participants and puts them in the conceptual frame of the solution-focused therapy model. For example, if a participant says, "I have a clearer idea of what I want to achieve in the coming time and which first small step I can take," the trainer can answer, "It is characteristic for the solution-focused approach to explore desired futures, contrary to the traditional therapy model that prefers to analyze problems."

Then the trainer asks the clients, "What have you noticed during this exercise? What have you experienced? What part of the exercise

Scale

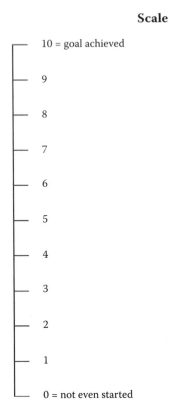

Figure 40.2 Goal scale.

was most useful to you?" Afterward, the trainer asks the same of the coaches. He or she invites the group to share as many experiences as possible and avoids arguing and rationalizations. The trainer welcomes every point of view; this helps to demonstrate and model solution-focused therapy.

41

TAKEN DRUGS

Ian Johnsen

PURPOSE

The acronym *TAKEN DRUGS* is used to draw together a set of practice principles—or tips, if you prefer—that are, in my view, somewhat essential in a solution-focused approach to working with people.

AUDIENCE

I have used this acronym with groups of professional people who may or may not have a lot of experience with applying principles of therapeutic practice in their work with clients. These people may not be therapists or psychologists, but coaches or consultants.

PROCESS

The acronym works well to prime solution-focused practice principles before reviewing a transcript or watching digital video. The audience then can really see or hear just how the principles come into play in the interaction between therapist and client. Facilitating some discussion of how the practice principles highlighted in the acronym were observed can be useful after using the transcript or video.

To start, I talk through each of the 10 points represented in the letters of the acronym and generally tell stories that highlight how the tip has made a difference in practice. For example, after reading out "take things at face value," I might talk about how hard this is to do in situations when we have some pressure to get to the truth of a matter or to establish "the facts"—particularly true when our job has a statutory and/or social control function. Also, in some therapy approaches, rather than taking something at face value, there is, in fact, a tendency to want to look behind or beneath the surface or apparent presentation of an issue. Instead of simply accepting what is said and utilising that, some other approaches presuppose that there is some underlying truth or more fundamental, hidden explanation.

I might tell one of the funny stories I get told by clients infuriated with psychoanalytic therapists who bring everything back to their relationship with their mother and then, when they become frustrated with this interpretation, use notions of transference to bring forth supposed further "truths." I talk about how, in a solution-focused approach, we try to stay on the surface and work with the presenting reality rather than second guessing or interpreting our client.

In relation to the second tip—to assume competence or good reasons for the clients' thinking, feeling, and action—I might hint that the transcript or digital video will probably show multiple instances and perhaps then tell a story. The story I sometimes tell is of 14-year-old David:

> David had run away from home and presented at a refuge in Sydney's red-light district of Kings Cross. The refuge phoned the child protection unit I worked in for assistance because David had said clearly, "I'm not going home and you can't make me." A colleague and I visited the refuge, where David adamantly repeated his assertion. Now, the reality was that many young people had been forcibly removed in this situation, with the police carrying them kicking and screaming into the back of a paddy wagon.
>
> Of course, this sort of interaction does not help to build rapport. If this young man were seriously at risk in some way and likely to resurface in our area, it would not be very helpful to engage like this and it is also very unpleasant and unskillful. So, rather than arguing the facts of the matter and pointing out the reality in situations such as his, I was able to take things at face value. I said to David, "Wow, you've obviously thought a lot about this."
>
> David said, "Whadya mean?"
>
> I said, "Well you sound really serious and you know leaving home's a big decision, so you must have really good reasons."
>
> David agreed; he said his dad was a "d###head" and he wasn't going to live with him. So we let David tell us a little about how his dad was a d###head and didn't challenge inconsistencies but just listened. Then I asked him whether he had thought about where he did want to live, whether he wanted to keep in touch with any of his family, what he did now that he liked to do or wanted to keep doing, and what about friends or going to the same school—was that important?
>
> "Whadya mean?" he asked. I explained that, given how serious it was, it sounded like he would need a long-term refuge, a place where he could stay for a couple of years at least. David thought about this a bit and told us about friends and what he liked, and

school, and then said he'd probably only need a place for a few months. I talked with my colleague and David about the medium-term refuges and the pros and cons, which ones had vacancies, which we thought were the best, and asked David what he thought about what we were saying.

David then said he thought he would need a place for only a few days or maybe he could stay at his mum's. We were able to talk that through, too, and to check what might be different between him and his dad after a few days. Eventually David decided that overnight would be all right and gave us permission to call his dad and talk to him about giving approval for a crisis refuge close to his home.

What we did in this situation was both to take what David said at face value and to assume that David had good reasons for doing what he was doing. In this case, the reality of David's situation took a little time to surface, but very often the search for the truth, especially at the beginning of working with someone, is so off the mark, it is actually counterproductive to try. On the way to the crisis placement, David told us that he had in fact skipped school that day, stolen his dad's car from the driveway, had the bad luck to be seen by his juvenile justice officer whilst driving his dad's car, and then, having returned the car and realising he was in deep strife, bolted before his dad got home!

After telling this story, I return to the next point in the acronym and tell another story or link it to some research, expand it in some way and/or invite the audience to speculate on how they find this point of use in their own work. The audience is then primed for a transcript or digital video.

TIME

The amount of time required depends on how many stories and bits of research and invitations for audience participation you want to give, leading up to a transcript or video example. In my work, I find 20–30 minutes is about right plus whatever piece of video or transcript I might want to use. Another 10–20 minutes can be used following the video or transcript for feedback and discussion around how the practice principle was evident.

MATERIALS

You need only the one page with the TAKEN DRUGS acronym, a stock of stories, some research points to support the tips, and a transcript and/or digital video showing a solution-focused approach. The ubiquitous butchers' paper can be used if you want small groups to discuss and then feed back their observations around the tips given in the acronym.

DEBRIEFING QUESTIONS

I point out that I am not making any claim that this set of points is conclusive or exclusive. That is to say, there may well be other sets of practice points that equally characterise a solution-focused approach and also that many other therapies may, more or less, share these principles. Facilitating some discussion of how the tips were evident in a transcript or video usually highlights how different people notice different aspects of interaction and is worthwhile.

TAKEN DRUGS!—10 TIPS FOR SOLUTION-FOCUSED PRACTICE

Sometimes your conversation will be so useful...other people will think that your client has TAKEN DRUGS!!!

Take things at face value.

Assume competence and good reasons for clients' feelings, thinking, actions, and interactions.

Keep the focus on clients' resources, coping in the present, and/or hopes for the future.

Expect that the change that the client wants from working with you will happen slowly.

Never be more enthusiastic for change than the client.

Don't give advice; instead, ask the client about her or his ideas and then ask about others' advice. (What would your mother/best friend say?)

Relay your respect for, interest in, and, as much as you can, understanding of the client's position.

Use only what the client is already doing or is already able to describe in detail in setting tasks or making suggestions at the end of your conversation.

Give compliments and plenty of affirmation in summation and in leading to task setting.

Start over if the conversation digresses—What does the client want? What is important to him or her? What else do you need to know in order to work together with the client in a way that is useful?

42

STUCK IN ISOMORPHISM AND COAXING THE WAY OUT
Via Less Dolorosa

Bruce Gorden

As supervisors, we are responsible that the case goes well and that the therapist does well, learns, and develops skill and know-how. I believe that clients and/or therapists are best convinced by their own words, so I am willing to go the extra mile for that to happen. Sometimes in group supervision, poignant learning opportunities present themselves, simply because the group is capable. Following is an example of the group becoming stuck like the therapist was stuck like the client was stuck. When mucking about in the mire of isomorphic process, there are some simple steps to free up all involved. Assume the therapist has the resources to succeed, and break the process down to doable steps.

A supervisee requests help for a case in which she feels "stuck." Her complaint is that nothing she does seems to help her client make progress. She wonders, now, whether she should refer the client to another therapist. In spite of her best efforts to help her client, she sees no progress. She has been complimenting her client for being tenacious and not giving up. Her client does keep coming back to therapy and complains bitterly how nothing helps, yet she feels a glimmer of hope because the therapist "is different from my previous therapists."

The supervision group members offer suggestions to the therapist that are rejected and compliments that are deflected because she sees no progress. She complains that she is not helping her client. She is complimented for being tenacious and not giving up. In spite of her own hopelessness, she admits that her client does feel some hope.

The isomorphic process is seen in the therapist's complaining in group, the client's complaining in therapy, and the group members "doing" what the therapist is "doing" in therapy: complimenting. The client and therapist appear stuck, unable to break out of a cycle of the "same damn thing" over and over again. Complimenting the client and complimenting the therapist don't seem to help.

The supervisor chooses to focus on the glimmer of hope. The assumption of the supervisor is that something the therapist is doing *is* working, and the therapist has the resources to put things to rights.

Supervisor: So, you sound really frustrated, and nothing you do seems to be helping your client.

Therapist: Yup.

Supervisor: And yet there is a glimmer of hope that keeps you going.

Therapist: [Sigh]…I guess.

Supervisor: What do you think it is that you do, which no other therapist has done, that gives your client a glimmer of hope?

Therapist: She says it's 'cause I listen to her.

Supervisor: So, something about how you listen to your client gives her a glimmer of hope.

Therapist: Yeah.

Supervisor: And the way you listen to your client is different from the way her previous therapists have listened to her.

Therapist: Yes, well, I show compassion.

Supervisor: OK, well, that is a big word. How would the members of this group know you were listening and showing compassion?

Therapist: Well, I accept her where she is, I don't make her [pensive pause]…Oh, my…I am trying to be like her other therapists. No wonder this isn't working. You know, when I am me and just listening and not trying to make something happen for her…that is what works. She has hope.

Group member: I am starting to have hope, too!!

Now the group has heuristic gain. This is a supervisor's joy, when we get to listen to supervisees connect theory with experience and develop ideas for further practice. The case goes well; the therapist develops experience and know-how.

43

SCALING PRACTICE

Heather Fiske

The goal of this exercise is to "flex the muscle" of putting questions into this useful form. I provide a short list of topics on a flip chart or slide, for example:

- watching TV
- politics (can specify U.S., Canadian, world, or local)
- dating
- winter
- cats and dogs
- physical exercise
- other (your choice)

In small groups (four to six people), participants take turns choosing a topic. The other group members then take turns discovering as much as they can about the first person's opinions and experiences regarding that topic, *using only scaling questions*. Debrief the experience, challenges, wording, uses, and applications of scaling.

44

A 10-MINUTE SOLUTION-FOCUSED
INTERVIEW TRAINING EXERCISE

Heather Fiske

(Inspired by Burns, 2008)

In general, I am leery of structured solution-focused interview formats because they omit the essential element of the client's response shaping the next question. However, we have to start somewhere!—and such formats do have a number of advantages:

- They give people new to SFBT an immediate, experiential sense or "flavour" of the work, different from what can be gained by learning solution-focused practice tools or from observing case examples.
- They can provide an initial grasp of the "flow" of solution-focused conversation, an aspect that can be a particular challenge for beginning and intermediate SFBT students.
- Short formats such as this one can make solution-focused conversation (as opposed to less integrated use of solution-focused questions or tools) seem accessible and possible for many practitioners who work outside the therapy room: in business, in shelter and street work, in schools, etc.

OUTLINE: A 10-MINUTE SOLUTION-FOCUSED CONVERSATION

- What are your best hopes?
- Suppose that you...[achieve those best hopes]. What will be different?
  - What else?
  - Who else will notice?
- On a scale from 1 to 10, if 10 stands for...[finish scaling question about person's goal]
  - Where are you now?
  - Where do you want to be?
  - What will be different when you are one step higher on the scale?
- What are you already doing that is on track?
  - What else are you doing that is on track?
- What is the next small step?
- Anything else?
- [Compliment]

REFERENCE

Burns, K. (2008). Ten minute talk: Using a solution-focused approach in supervision. *Solution News, 3*(3), 8–10.

45

WORKPLACE TRAINING EXERCISES

Heather Fiske

COMMON GROUND

Participants think of a colleague with whom they find interaction difficult. They do not have to identify the person or the nature of the difficulty. Participants are then asked to list in 3 minutes as many ways as possible that they have something in common with this person. Lists are read aloud and the exercise is debriefed using questions such as:

- On a scale from 1 to 10, with 10 meaning dead easy and 1 meaning very difficult, how difficult was it to make a list?
- What did you notice as you listened to other people's lists?
- How could this exercise be useful for you?
- What difference might it make to do or review this exercise with yourself before a meeting or interaction that you think could be difficult?

AN EXPERIENCE OF TEAMWORK

In small groups, participants take turns interviewing one another using the following questions:

- Describe an occasion when you knew you were part of a team.
- How did you contribute?
- How did others contribute?

- How did they contribute to your contribution?
- How did you contribute to their contribution?

Debrief regarding common threads, perceptions, and unique contributions.

46

FOUR CONSTRUCTIVE CONVERSATIONS

Heather Fiske

CONSTRUCTIVE CONVERSATION ONE[1]

Person A plays a surly teenager; Person B plays a counselor. The teen identifies a problem and the counselor suggests a reasonable solution. In the first condition, the counselor begins with, "What you should do is…." In the second condition, the counselor begins with, "I wonder what would happen if you…." Debrief with questions about the difference, beginning with the teenager's point of view.

CONSTRUCTIVE CONVERSATION TWO

Person A discusses (his or her own, real) plans for an upcoming vacation or time off; Person B listens and seeks more information. In the first condition, B begins every inquiry or statement with, "But…." In the second condition, B begins every inquiry or statement with, "And…."[2] Debrief the differences.

CONSTRUCTIVE CONVERSATION THREE

Person A discusses his or her (own, real) way of conducting some everyday life activity (how I cook, get my kids up in the morning, drive to work, walk my dog, get exercise, etc.). Person B listens and asks for details. In the first condition, B begins each question with, "Why?"

In the second condition, Person B begins each question with, "How?" Debrief the differences.

Alternative: Person A discusses his or her resolution of a problem or issue.

CONSTRUCTIVE CONVERSATION FOUR

Person A identifies a real problem or issue (perhaps work related, perhaps minor; something that is comfortable for the person to discuss). Person B asks questions about what will be different or better when the issue is resolved or improved. Each question B asks must begin with, "Suppose…" or "When you…." Debrief with questions about the effects and usefulness of these phrasings.

NOTES

1. I have also thought and talked about this expanding, work-in-progress series of exercises as "making talk work" or just "tinkering with language," which I see as essentially solution-focused activities.
2. I tried varying the order of these conditions, but one participant wailed that the "but" conversation had ruined her vacation!

47

DESCRIPTION, REFLECTION, SPECULATION

Ian Johnsen

PURPOSE

The description, reflection, speculation (DRS) chart is part of a set of tools that I find useful in introducing a solution-focused approach. The chart sometimes seems more useful in cases where people are first more familiar with other approaches. A thumbnail sketch of similarities and differences among approaches, the chart helps people to locate solution-focused practice within their broader understanding.

AUDIENCE

The idea is probably most suited to those who are not already comfortable with where a solution-focused approach sits within other family therapy approaches and where it sits more broadly among approaches to working with people that are informed by therapeutic practice principles. I use it in training with people who work with people in a variety of contexts: caseworkers, youth workers, those workers who engage in various capacities with "at risk" populations, and also sometimes with social workers or psychologists who are not familiar with such an approach.

Most learning involves engaging in a process of description, reflection, and speculation, but we conceive of these elements of this process very differently depending on our overarching frame—how we understand the construction of knowledge. Whilst all types of learning or knowledge construction have similarities, the process of learning is different depending on our frame. Different types of knowledge may be more or less suited to different frames.

PROCESS

The DRS chart (Figure 47.1) can be used in itself as a tool in introducing a solution-focused approach. However, I find it most useful as part of a training day exercise that looks at the beginning (description) phase of an interaction or interview, the middle (reflection) stage of an interaction or interview, and the ending (speculation) phase of an interaction or interview. In this situation, participants in the training day can be asked to work in small groups and to identify a workplace interaction or interview that might be useful to think more about. The group takes the scene, the phases of the interaction or interview, and unpacks it, discussing the pattern of interaction that typically occurs, which may often but not necessarily be problem focused.

The next step is then to unpack the same scene supposing a solution-focused approach and thereby highlighting possible different types of questions and interaction. If we worked from within a solution-focused frame, what might happen at the beginning/description, the middle/reflection, and the ending/speculation stages with a case example such as theirs? How is using a solution-focused approach the same as or different from using another or problem-focused approach?

I find it is more practical to do this contrasting with a solution-focused approach as a large group because smaller groups might need more time or coaching than one can provide in a busy training schedule.

TIME

It takes around 10 minutes for an overview of the chart. In a larger group, participants can be invited to give examples of general starting, middle, and end points in the approach they most commonly use, so more time can be taken. The contrasting approaches exercise takes 20–40 minutes, depending on the number of small groups within a larger group and the level of detail given for each stage of the interaction. I have used it with groups of 24 (six small groups of four) and in a team format with six to eight people. If one example finishes quickly, another can be taken, although sometimes one example can be done more slowly and thoroughly.

	Problem-Focused	Psychodynamic	Cognitive/Behavioural	Narrative	Strengths-Based	Solution-Focused
Description	What is wrong?	What intra- or inter-personal history is the problem embedded in?	What faulty thinking leads to problem occurring?	What is the dominant story and how does my story relate?	What skills and strengths are already present or might assist?	What do I/we hope for in this context?
Reflection	Why? What is the underlying cause?	How can we understand this and achieve insight?	How realistic is that way of thinking?	What other/alternative story fits my experience and desires?	How did I develop this skill? How do I utilise this resource now?	What already works toward that? How did that happen? What else?
Speculation	How do we fix that?	How can this insight guide growth and development?	What is a better/more realistic way to think?	How can I embrace and develop that story?	How can I further utilise resources? What would the outcome be?	How will we know we are moving further toward our hopes?

Figure 47.1 The DRS chart.

MATERIALS

Materials required include the DRS chart, butchers' paper and/or white boards and markers, and contrasting exercise pages. The paper is divided into two columns over two pages divided by three rows. The columns can be titled, "typical statements/interventions or questions," and then, "most probable client responses." The rows are the beginning/description, the middle/reflection, and the ending/speculation stages of working with a client.

If working in small groups within a larger group, using butchers' paper and asking for some examples of interaction from case experience at each stage can be helpful. With just a small team, the process is similar but can be a brainstorming session using a white board (or, better, two) divided into six parts.

DEBRIEFING QUESTIONS

From my point of view, the advantage of a solution-focused frame is that at every step of learning, we tap motivation. In describing shared hoped-for outcomes, we are able to invite hope and promote ownership of the process of learning. In reflecting on what is working and how, we activate resources and affirm. In speculating on the future, we clarify the next steps toward the fulfilment of our desired outcome.

That said, I think it is important to point out that, in advocating for this approach, I am not saying that a solution-focused approach is necessarily the right approach and another approach is somehow less right or wrong. It is, of course, very important to validate and affirm the work that is already being done by people and, although I advocate for such things as enhanced goal definition, motivation, and rapport building in using a solution-focused approach, all types of successful work already tap these aspects.

I have introduced the DRS chart by saying it is certainly not an adequate representation of any framework, but rather a loose starting point in thinking about some of the similarities and differences in different ways of working with people. I also point out that although I relate the beginning, middle, and end stages of interaction to engaging in a process of describing, reflecting, and speculating, these processes are not necessarily discrete and tied only to one stage of interaction; human communication is generally much messier than a model allows. To paraphrase (I believe) Brian Cade, "We want only to date our model, not marry it."

48

THE WORST THINGS YOU COULD EVER HEAR IN A THERAPY HOUR

Bruce Gorden

This is an exercise that is beneficial for almost any level of therapist. I have done this in supervision groups with a mix of trainees, interns, and licensed professionals. The idea is to generate any number of difficult situations a therapist could encounter in a therapy hour. This can be fun as well as giving therapists a sigh of relief. During problem generation, many are relieved because other therapists worry about these things too.

After generating the list of difficulties, we brainstorm. Any idea is considered when we generate potential therapeutic responses to problem scenarios. The following are a few examples of "worst fears" and therapeutic response candidates. The intent is to equip therapists to be ready to respond in a helpful manner when surprising, anxiety-provoking, or just plain uncomfortable moments happen during a therapy hour. I hope you can expand the list of problems and potentially helpful responses.

Difficulty: Client says, "You suck as a therapist."
Potential responses:
- On a scale from 0 to 10, where would you place me now?
- If I sucked just a little less, how would you respond as a client?
- What will you be doing in therapy when I don't suck?
- How will I know when you think I suck less?

Difficulty: Client says, "When I leave here today, I am going to kill myself."

This is a serious subject and we spend a good deal of time on it. We refer the reader to Fiske's (2008) book, *Hope in Action: Solution-Focused Conversations About Suicide.* On page 6, Fiske lists practice principles for suicide intervention. Following are just a few from that list:

- Utilize what the client brings.
- Focus on reasons for living.
- Make every encounter therapeutic. Contain crisis.
- Tap into hope.

Also, on page 48 is a list of example questions about reasons for living:

- What are your reasons for living?
- What is your most important reason for living?
- What keeps you going?
- What helps you fight back?

We were all taught to assess for lethality, but we weren't taught to assess for life. Here are some other questions we generated:

- Who will be most devastated by losing you?
- If you could hear people talk after you are gone, what would you hope to hear them say?
- What do you think St. Peter will say to you?
- I have never had a client with so much passion about something. What else are you passionate about?

Difficulty: Client says, "You have not done one thing to help me."
Potential responses:
  - What were some things I did that were almost helpful to you?
  - If I did say something that helped you, how would you respond?
  - Have you been able to get a therapist to do something helpful previously?

Difficulty: Client says, "You are not worth the price you charge."
Potential responses:
  - What do you think is a fair amount?
  - What would you need to believe x to be a fair amount?
  - If I did more than that, could I charge more?

- Has there been a time recently when you thought the price was fair?

Difficulty: Client says, "You obviously don't care about me."
Potential responses:
- How would the observation team know that I cared about you?
- How would your life be different if you knew I cared about you?
- What could I do right now that would let you know I care about you?
- Do you think I could be of help to you even if I didn't care?

Difficulty: Client says, "I am really attracted to you right now."
Potential responses:
- Thank you.
- Thank you. Of course, you know that my code of ethics states that sex is never a part of the therapeutic relationship.
- I assume you have a really good reason for me to know you are attracted to me right now.
- Yeah, I get that a lot.
- What would you like to be able to say to me after this moment passes?

We think it would be cool if we had an international pool of potential problems and helpful responses to draw from. Perhaps this is a beginning.

REFERENCE

Fiske, H. (2008). *Hope in action: Solution-focused conversations about suicide.* New York: Routledge.

49

EVIDENCE-BASED SUPERVISION

Identifying Successful Moments of
Solution-Focused Brief Therapy

Sara A. Smock

INTRODUCTION

During my work on a research project with Janet Beavin Bavelas, I discovered that microanalyzing therapy videotapes had several functions. Microanalysis, a type of analysis developed by Bavelas, is a "close examination of actual communication sequences" (Bavelas, McGee, Phillips, & Routledge, 2000, p. 47). I quickly discovered that this type of analysis could be used as a tool for trainers, especially SFBT trainers. Because SFBT values the importance of language in therapy, microanalysis seems to be a perfect medium for training trainees in the model.

So I began to use the process of microanalysis in training individuals in SFBT. At first, I was unsure how to transfer this research approach specifically to supervision, but it fell right into place. While there can be multiple uses of microanalysis for training and research, I would like to share one activity with you.

DESCRIPTION OF THE INTERVENTION

Preparation for the Activity

Before your next supervision meeting, ask your student/trainee to do a little prep work. Begin by asking your student/trainee to review several of their clinical videos where they are using SFBT. Ask them to select a tape that shows their best SFBT session. Next, have your student/trainee select a 5-minute clip of the video that they especially like.

Activity

When you meet with your trainee, watch the selected 5-minute clip. After watching the clip together, you should identify moments in the clip where you noticed the trainee's success in using the model. This will probably require watching the video a few times to pinpoint those exact moments of success. Moments can be part of an utterance (i.e., talking turn in the dialogue) or an entire utterance. A new moment can begin once the dialogue returns to the therapist. You could consider every utterance within the 5-minute clip as a success or just a few.

It is helpful to record the specific places where successful moments occur as you review the clip with your student/trainee. If you are using a DVD player or a VCR, use the tracking device to note these moments. If the video is an MPEG file, you can download ELAN (a free program used to view MPEG videos) from http://www.mpi.nl/tools/ to track the occurrences using ELAN's precise minute/second counter. Keep track of the exact moments by recording the start and stop times. For example, if the moment is an entire utterance and the utterance begins at 4:35 and lasts until 4:55, you would record 4:35–4:55. Marking the precise moments of success (whether they are an entire utterance or a part of an utterance) is important.

Once the examples of successful SFBT moments are identified, watch just the selected parts. As both of you are watching these moments, develop a list of things (evidence) that the trainee is doing. "Evidence" includes, but is not limited to, the following: tone of voice, the phrasing of utterances, posture, nonverbals, inflection, the content, etc. Be very specific and detailed about what the trainee is doing that illustrates proper use of SFBT. You and the trainee should work together to identify the evidence. Once the list of evidence is determined, you and your trainee can use this list in future supervision sessions to detect successful use of SFBT in other videos.

In addition to using the evidence list to highlight the trainee's successes, you can ask the following questions about the times when the trainee is displaying evidence:

1. What did the client do/say right before the evidence occurred?
2. How did the client respond after the evidence occurred?
3. What was helpful about this exercise?
4. How will this exercise help you to display more evidence in the future?

Example of Using This Activity   Trainees may find this activity challenging because they are nervous about analyzing their own videos. If you notice that your student/trainee is anxious about this activity or claims not to have a "good" videotape, encourage the trainee to select the best video (best—not perfect) from the collection. Reassure the trainee that this exercise is meant to highlight their successes, not to criticize them on their use of SFBT.

So what happens if your trainee is too nervous to do this activity? If reassuring your trainee that this would be a helpful exercise doesn't work, offer to use one of your own video clips to review. You can use the same process with your clip (or a clip from a published SFBT video) to do this exercise. The goal is to help trainees identify SFBT in action; the details of the exercise can and should be altered to fit the needs of your trainee.

What happens if your trainee brings a video clip that doesn't show use of SFBT? This is a very good question. During the training process, it is possible that trainees still struggle with using SFBT. If you watch the clip with your trainee and have difficulty finding moments of success, try this alternative. Tell your trainee that there are times when they *start* to use SFBT successfully and you want to look at these instances more closely. Find precise moments when the trainee *starts* to use SFBT effectively. Even if it is as small as nonverbal communication or tone of voice, you can find something that supports the tenets of SFBT.

Replay those moments with your trainee and ask them how they would make the moment *more* solution focused. Have a dialogue with your trainee about possible options that would make this moment *more* solution-focused. Remember to highlight *any* evidence of successful SFBT while dialoguing about ways to improve the moment. Normalize for your trainee that even seasoned solution-focused therapists would reword parts of their session to make them *more* solution focused. The goal of this exercise is to identify successes (even small successes) and dialogue about what could make work better in the future.

CONCLUSION AND CONTRAINDICATIONS

There are several goals of this exercise. First and foremost, the goal is to help trainees recognize successes in their use of SFBT. Although identifying the evidence of their success is important, it is *also* important to dialogue about how they would like to see their use of SFBT improve in the future. Another goal is to help trainees identify SFBT in action. Whether they are analyzing their own videos or watching Steve or Insoo, identifying the evidence of successful SFBT is important.

While this activity can be altered for the various needs of trainees, some contraindications do exist. If a trainee is new to SFBT, it may be difficult for them to identify evidence of successful SFBT in video clips, so this activity would not be recommended. In addition, if you have trainees that would use this activity for self-defeating purposes (i.e., would use this activity to confirm that they don't understand SFBT), this activity would not be appropriate.

REFERENCE

Bavelas, J. B., McGee, D., Phillips, B., & Routledge, R. (2000). Microanalysis of communication in psychotherapy. *Human Systems: The Journal of Systemic Consultation & Management, 11,* 47–66.

50

TRAINING THERAPISTS FOR SFBT GROUP WORK
A Multidimensional Approach

Adam S. Froerer and Sara A. Smock

INTRODUCTION

This training exercise was developed at a marriage and family therapy (MFT) training clinic as part of a graduate practicum course. The practicum consisted of both master's and doctoral students preparing to conduct solution-focused brief therapy (SFBT) groups. Students began the training course with varying degrees of exposure to and interest in SFBT. We will share our experiences of this training from both the trainee's and the trainer's perspective. Adam Froerer, AF, was a doctoral student with considerable interest in using SFBT as his primary model. Sara Smock, SS, serves as a trainer of SFBT and is always looking for new and innovative ways to teach SFBT.

PURPOSE OF THE EXERCISE

The purpose of this training exercise is to provide a description of one multidimensional approach with accompanying examples of training therapists to use solution-focused therapy in a group format.

TRAINING SCHEDULE

We find this training to be useful when completed in six 1-hour sessions over a 6-week period of time. The schedule can and should be modified to meet the needs of your training group.

Week 1: Overview of SFBT

During the first week, the trainer provides an overview of SFBT. In this portion of the training, a PowerPoint presentation and handouts on the basics of SFBT are used. Materials can include information explaining the SFBT philosophy, a delineation of problem solving versus solution building, and the core assumptions of SFBT. The information to be included in the presentation can be obtained from books and articles written by the developers, Steve de Shazer and Insoo Kim Berg, and others (cf. De Jong & Berg, 2007; de Shazer 1988, 1991, 1993, 1994). The goal of week 1 is to present and discuss the underlying principles and philosophy of SFBT before discussion interventions. The information is presented while inviting questions from trainees. The depth of the presentation should vary depending on the trainees' level of experience.

Following are some discussion questions that can be used along with the didactic presentation:

1. Can SFBT be helpful long term if an SFBT therapist doesn't focus on the problem?
2. How do issues of diversity get incorporated within an SFBT session?
3. Why is language so important in SFBT sessions?
4. Do SFBT therapists really consider language to be reality?

AF: As a trainee, I liked getting the foundational information first. I was familiar with SFBT before this training exercise, but it was nice to have a refresher on what the philosophy of SFBT is before being required to do therapy from this model.

Week 2: Interventions

The second week of the training should also be composed of didactic information, but should focus on SFBT interventions. Again, a PowerPoint presentation and handouts with explanations of each intervention are used. Additionally, examples are given of how the intervention could be worded and used. The interventions in the presentation or on the handouts should include:

1. The miracle question
2. Scaling questions

3. Difference questions
4. Relational questions
5. Exception questions
6. Taking a break
7. Giving compliments
8. Assigning homework

The trainer should cover each of these interventions in detail and should encourage discussion and questions from the trainees. The goal of week 2 is to familiarize the participants with SFBT interventions and increase their comfort levels in using these interventions in therapy sessions. Consideration should be given to the different learning styles of the trainees.

To make the interventions more real and understandable to the participants, video illustrations from the founders/experts of the SFBT can be used. This allows the trainees to see the interventions in action. The videos can be purchased from the Solution-Focused Brief Therapy Association (www.sfbta.org). Additionally, the trainer can show clips of other therapeutic models (particularly cognitive behavioral therapy and motivational interviewing) as a way to highlight similarities and differences.

These comparison models appear to be similar to SFBT on a surface level. By showing clips from comparison models, the specific similarities and differences between these models and SFBT can be highlighted. These comparison videos can be purchased from the American Psychological Association (www.apa.org). The trainer can also facilitate a discussion about how language is important in SFBT.

Another way to conclude this training session is to have the participants role-play in dyads the various interventions illustrated during the session. The trainer should be available to observe, answer questions, and provide feedback on the use and language of the intervention implementation.

AF: As a trainee, I liked having other models to compare to SFBT. It solidified for me what is part of the SFBT model and what isn't. This helped me feel like I understood how to use the model much better.

Week 3: Group Work

The goal of week 3 is to apply the philosophy and interventions learned in previous weeks to SFBT groups. During this week, trainees spend time watching videos of therapists conducting SFBT groups. While the group is watching the video, the trainer stops the session regularly to point out how the SFBT tenets and interventions are being incorporated within the group session and creates a discussion about other possible directions the group therapists in the video could have gone while still remaining solution focused. In addition, trainees can brainstorm other questions or interventions the therapists from the videos could have used that would have been appropriate within given situations.

AF: As a trainee, watching the videos of other therapists completing SFBT groups helped me feel encouraged that I possess the skills and knowledge necessary to be an effective group facilitator. I really enjoyed having discussions about alternative questions that could be used. It was also helpful to know there isn't just one right way to lead an SFBT group.

Week 4: Microanalysis of Group Work

During week 4, a method called microanalysis is used to further highlight unique distinctions of SFBT. Microanalysis is a "close examination of actual communication sequences" (Bavelas, McGee, Phillips, & Routledge, 2000, p. 47). Generally, microanalysis is used as a research method, but it is growing in popularity as a training method (see the example of using microanalysis for training in Chapter 49). The goal of using microanalysis as part of the training is to solidify the importance of language within SFBT sessions and to give trainees a chance to look carefully at language and word choice.

For this activity, trainees watch small sections of SFBT videos by the founders of/experts in SFBT focusing specifically on the therapist's use of language. Future-oriented and strength-based language utilized by the therapist is highlighted by the trainer. In addition, times when the therapist uses the client's language when formulating a response are highlighted. Microanalysis can be used as a springboard to discuss SFBT language. Emphasis should be placed on context and looking at language as it develops in sequences of interchange between the client and the therapist.

AF: As a trainee, using microanalysis helped me become more conscious of the language I use in therapy and helped me understand what I choose to focus on. Microanalysis also helped me realize how the language I use in session influences the direction of therapy.

Week 5: Role-Play

During week 5, trainees get their first chance to apply their training. The goal of this week is to provide hands-on practice and identify areas of strength and areas of growth. During this week, trainees use the session outline as a guide to do a role-play of an SFBT group (see the end of this chapter for the session outline). The role-play consists of two trainees serving as the therapists and the remainder of the trainees acting as clients. During the role-play, the trainer pauses when necessary for instruction/clarification or for questions from the participants.

AF: As a trainee, I think this week was the most helpful to prepare for facilitating a group session. It helped to identify areas where I felt comfortable and areas where I was uncertain. After this exercise, I now feel more confident to lead an SFBT group. In my talking with the other trainees, they indicated that they also really like role-playing a group and think it is the most helpful piece of the training.

Week 6: Role-Play Continued

In week 6, trainees get a second opportunity to role-play facilitating an SFBT group. Before this role-play exercise, the trainer asks the trainees to discuss questions from the previous week's experience. It is important to make sure all trainees get a chance to be one of the co-therapists. During this last session, the trainer interjects comments much less and relies on the trainees to ask questions about things they are unsure of. The training is concluded with a final question-and-answer period.

AF: Again, as a trainee, I found weeks 5 and 6 to be the most helpful sessions of the training. The firsthand experience coupled with the immediate feedback from the trainer was very helpful in learning how to relate my knowledge of SFBT to practical application. At the conclusion of the training, my fellow trainees also said that their knowledge and comfort level in using SFBT had increased.

CONCLUSION AND CONTRAINDICATIONS

The purpose of this training exercise is to teach and train new therapists to understand and use SFBT in group therapy. The trainees learn through didactic training, observing others, analyzing the language of SFBT, and applying their knowledge through role-plays. We feel that using multiple methods of training gives trainees opportunities to learn based on their individual learning styles.

Despite our positive experience of this training format, there may be some contraindications. First, this training format is ideal for experienced therapists and may not be helpful, developmentally, for beginning therapists. Second, some members of the trainee group may not be motivated to learn SFBT and may distract other, interested trainees. In this case, it is important for the trainer to address this individually with the trainee. Finally, because trainees may sometimes feel self-conscious being the therapist in the role-plays, ask for volunteers to serve as the therapists. Always be clear with trainees that role-plays are mere exercises and "perfect" use of the model is not expected.

REFERENCES

Bavelas, J. B., McGee, D., Phillips, B., & Routledge, R. (2000). Microanalysis of communication in psychotherapy. *Human Systems: The Journal of Systemic Consultation & Management, 11,* 47–66.

De Jong, P., & Berg, I. K. (2007). *Interviewing for solutions* (3rd ed.). Pacific Grove, CA: Brooks/Cole.

de Shazer, S. (1988). *Clues: Investigating solutions in brief therapy.* New York: W. W. Norton.

de Shazer, S. (1991). *Putting difference to work.* New York: W. W. Norton.

de Shazer, S. (1993). Creative misunderstanding: There is no escape from language. In S. Gilligan & R. Price (Eds.), *Therapeutic conversations.* New York: W. W. Norton.

de Shazer, S. (1994). *Words were originally magic.* New York: W. W. Norton.

APPENDIX: RESOURCES

Articles on Microanalysis

Bavelas, J. B., McGee, D., Phillips, B., & Routledge, R. (2000). Microanalysis of communication in psychotherapy. *Human Systems: The Journal of Systemic Consultation & Management, 11,* 47–66.

McGee, D., Del Vento, A., & Bavelas, J. B. (2005). An interactional model of questions as therapeutic interventions. *Journal of Marital and Family Therapy, 31*(4), 371–384.

Tomori, C., & Bavelas, J. B. (2007). Using microanalysis of communication to compare solution-focused and client-centered therapies. *Journal of Family Psychotherapy, 18*(3), 25–43.

Shortened Outline of the Session Format

1. Ask group members to report on the successes achieved during the previous week.

2. Ask the group members an introduction question—for example, "What would your family members tell me is the most important quality you have?"

3. Group leader(s) identify a theme (e.g., hope, confidence, optimism, etc.) from the responses to the previous question and reflect this theme back to the group members. Group leader(s) ask the group members permission to address this theme unless there are emergencies that need to be addressed.

4. Group leaders ask the group the miracle question or other future-oriented question based on the theme—for example, "If you have more (hope, confidence, optimism) 1 year from now, how has that helped you to achieve your miracle?"
5. Group leaders listen for and help identify exceptions to the problem.
6. Ask a scaling question to determine the client's current level of progress toward his or her goal and find out what the client has done to achieve his or her current level—for example, "You gave yourself a 3. How did you manage to get yourself to a 3 already?"
7. Connect group members' struggles, goals, and successes with each other as a way to support and model solutions.
8. Take a break.
9. Ask group members how the theme applies to them individually.
10. Offer compliments.
11. Invite the group members to assign themselves homework for the upcoming week and then group adjourns.

51

PSYCHIATRY SHOULD BE A PARENTHESIS IN PEOPLE'S LIVES

Harry Korman

On the phone, she started by saying: "You're my last hope. He tried to kill himself twice last week. Everyone has given up." She then told the story: Her 20-year-old son had been in a car accident 6 months earlier and would never walk again. After 6 months of rehabilitation, he was now back to living with his parents, physically as well as he could be but mentally, not at all. "Can you please see him? You're our last hope—he has so much to live for."

The doorbell rang and she was there with him in his wheelchair. She said to us, "I'll be back in an hour," and before I had the time to respond, she was in the elevator on her way down and Michael wheeled himself into my office.

Name, address, phone number, permission to tape, and I see on the videotape that I'm settling in—drawing a line on the paper and saying:

Okay...Your mother phoned yesterday...What did she tell me...? Car accident in September...Paralyzed from the chest down...Do you have full strength in your arms?

Yes.

How high is it?

Th8

Hmm. Hmm. She also said you wanted to live?

Mother had said on the phone, "He has so much to live for," so I am not really lying, just pushing my understanding of what she said a bit. I am also thinking that since he is alive and has come to my office, there must be some will to live somewhere despite the look on his face and the multiple suicide attempts.

That I wanted...?

To live—that's what she told me.

An almost sardonic smile appears as he responds:

Live happily if so...

I repeat: *"Live happily?"* and he responds "Yes," and then adds with some emphasis, "not like this." I check again: *"Live happily and not like this?"* and he acknowledges that I understood correctly with a brief yes.

There is a 14-second pause as I look up, rocking slowly in my chair, looking as if I'm thinking, and he looks intently at me waiting for me to continue. So he wants to live happily. Could that be a working project for therapy, something that is important to him, something I want to work with him on, and something that could possibly happen as a result of our talking? Does *he* think it's possible?

"Do you think it's possible?"

"I really don't know," he answers, and there is a short pause before he continues: "I wish I knew. And I wish I knew when, because I really can't take waiting any longer." There is bitterness in his voice.

"So you don't know if it's possible and you don't know when?"

He confirms that I understood: "Precisely."

There is a 10-second pause while I'm thinking about an old brief therapy rule: "When in doubt, be conservative." His not knowing if it's possible means we can't start building a preferred future on "living happily" and I can't ask the miracle question yet. "I don't know" means he doesn't know and Michael and I have to figure out another working project. So I start over.

"I want to say first that I understood from your mother that you wanted help, you wanted to try...and I think it's a good idea to seek help when one feels as badly as you do. Two suicide attempts, if I understood your mother correctly...I also want to say that there are no guarantees that this will be of any help. The only thing I can guarantee is that I will do my best and I assume you will too. That is obvious and then we'll see how it turns out."

I look at my notes and continue:

"So—live happily and not like this—What would be something...that was different in what you felt, thought, or did today or tomorrow after our conversation that was some indication to you that this session had not been a complete waste of your time?"

Michael thinks about this question for almost 15 seconds before answering, "If I felt like coming back again, that would be a good sign."

I smile and nod and *repeat, "So – if you feel like coming back that would be **one sign** for you? What else?"* and I emphasize *one sign* because I am not going to tell him that I will not use this as a working project because I need a project that has to do with life outside therapy, which is also why I ask, "What else?" I also smile because I'm reminded of this old doctor at my first job as a doctor who told me about the two guidelines that had helped him through many years of medicine and that have now guided me for more years than I care to remember: "Most diseases heal despite the treatment" and "The primary purpose of the health care system is to create a need for health care."

I am also thinking about the motto I tried to introduce into child psychiatry some 15 years ago: "We want to do everything we can to make psychiatry a parenthesis in people's lives."

Building on, making "if I felt like coming back again" the first step in the solution-building process would mean going against these ideas because it is about therapy instead of life outside therapy.

I have used this tape many times in teaching and I often stop at this point and ask people whether we have a common project, a working project, and most people think we have a beginning of one and I don't disagree with them. Wanting to come back could be an expression of having some hope that things could improve and it would probably have been easy to move the dialogue into daily activities of the client's life where expressions of this hope could be noticed by the client and the people close to him. But Michael's statement in itself does not contain any of this; it only stated that feeling like wanting to come back would be a good sign.

Michael took another 3 minutes to come up with something that would be different and a sign of the session's having been helpful:

"Not only feeling positive about coming here again—but also feeling positive about something else—something small...anything."

I answered, *"And with anything, you really mean anything."* He said, "Yes," and I answered, *"So that's how tough things are right now."* He said, "Yes," and I added, *"Bloody hell!...Bloody hell!"* He looked at me, perhaps for the first time in the session, and said, "Yes, those are the right words for it."

I asked him in what area of his life he would first start noticing "if he started feeling something positive about anything" and he answered that he might be able to look himself in the mirror and he might smile toward his mother, perhaps even wholeheartedly, and his mother would probably notice and she would probably smile back at him.

Normally, I don't ask people what we should talk about or what we need to do in the session. I think every question contains presuppositions and I don't want to pretend things I can't stand for like the client's deciding on how we are going to talk about things. I know that my first sessions with clients almost always contain the miracle question and I have yet to meet a client who would answer, "I want to talk about how my life would be different the day after a miracle that happened while I slept solved the problem that brought me here." I also think that talking about what happens in therapy diverts attention away from the business at hand, which is to talk about how the client wants to "be in the world" and what parts of this are already happening. Therapy is talking about life, not talking about therapy.

So, working for psychiatry/therapy to be a parenthesis in people's lives means not only doing as little as possible, but also not spanning bridges between sessions, such as, "So, last time you were here we talked about…." What happens in therapy should never be an important subject in the therapy sessions. It's what happens between the sessions that contains what is important to talk about.

52

WHEN THE CLIENT DOESN'T FOLLOW THE SCRIPT

Joel Simon

Two of the main principles inherent in solution-focused practice follow Milton Erickson's concepts of cooperation and utilization. *Cooperation* essentially means accepting and working within the client's reality (Gilligan, 1987). *Utilization* means that no matter what the client says, it is to be accepted as a useful response and the therapist's next intervention should be built upon that response.

Steve de Shazer (personal communication, July 18, 1994) once stated that solution focus is simple therapy, but simple does not mean easy. Solution-focused practice is relatively easy when the client responds in predictable ways. However, when the client provides the therapist with the unexpected response, it is all too easy—especially for the novice solution-focused practitioner—to forget the concepts of cooperation and utilization and revert to more comfortable (albeit less useful) problem-focused techniques.

As a solution-focused trainer, I have often thought of exercises that might help therapists to practice cooperation and utilization, and help them to find ways to maintain a solution-building focus in the face of the unpredictable. After all, the unpredictable response ultimately provides an opportunity for learning that the otherwise predictable does not. It was with this goal in mind that the exercise "When the Client Does Not Follow the Script" was first introduced at the SFBTA 2008 Conference on Solution-Focused Practices in Austin, Texas.

MATERIALS AND SETUP

For the exercise, the following are needed:

- three sheets of paper, each divided and cut into squares numbered 1 through 25
- easel or white board with appropriate markers
- two containers to hold the numbered squares
- laptop and projector with speakers
- video scenarios

VIDEO SCENARIOS

For this exercise, I videotaped 25 scenarios. I began by working with a group of colleagues who had been trained in solution-focused practice. We brainstormed a number of possible scenarios, most of which one or more of the group had experienced. Using a camcorder, we then recorded the various scenarios, each one averaging less than a minute. Each scenario is then assigned a number. Table 52.1 is a listing of those video examples.

A word about number 25 in the table is probably appropriate. While the client responses in the table appear to range from the sublime to the ridiculous, in fact conversations similar to the final scenario, while perhaps rarer, do happen. I recall one such case when I asked a client the question how the session might be useful. He informed me that he had moved from Massachusetts to New York state to put distance between himself and the devil. We spent the rest of the session talking about other ways in which he is able to keep safe.

The videos can either be burned to a CD-R in a Windows Media Player (.wmp) or similar format, or saved directly to a laptop's hard drive. It is best to burn each scenario as a separate file named only by its sequence number.

PROCEDURE

Assuming at least 25 participants, each is given a numbered square. The other two sets are placed in separate containers. Two numbers are drawn from the first container. The first person who responds is designated the therapist and the second person the client. A number is drawn from the second container and the related number of the scenario is played. The therapist is assured that at any time, he or she can stop the role-play and ask for suggestions from the other workshop participants. These suggestions should be listed on the easel or white board. The therapist can then choose one of the interventions and proceed.

Table 52.1 Therapist Questions and Client Responses

No.	Therapist Question	Client Response
1	So, that's my question: What will be different tomorrow that will tell you this miracle happened?	I don't believe in miracles.
2	So, how will you know that our meeting together had been useful for you?	Well, my husband died back in April.
3	When you wake up, how will you know this miracle happened?	My deceased husband would be sleeping next to me.
4	When you wake up, how will you know this miracle happened?	This would all be a bad dream.
5	When you wake up, how will you know this miracle happened?	I have no idea.
6	When you wake up, how will you know this miracle happened?	I haven't had a good thing happen to me since I can't remember when.
7	When you wake up, how will you know this miracle happened?	I really never sleep.
8	When you wake up, how will you know this miracle happened?	My mind is so full of crap I wouldn't know anything different had happened!
9	Let's suppose that our meeting together is helpful to you. How will you know that our time together has been useful?	Oh, my husband would stop drinking.
10	Let's suppose that our meeting together is helpful to you. How will you know that our time together has been useful?	You know this is not my idea to come here. It's my wife's idea.
11	Let's suppose that our meeting together is helpful to you. How will you know that our time together has been useful?	I really need to have you understand what happened to me.
12	Let's suppose that our meeting together is helpful to you. How will you know that our time together has been useful?	I don't think it can be. I think that this is the way it's always been.
13	Let's suppose that our meeting together is helpful to you. How will you know that our time together has been useful?	I need to vent!
14	So what will tell you that our time together is done?	Done? Are you dumping me? Already?

(continued)

Table 52.1 Therapist Questions and Client Responses (continued)

No.	Therapist Question	Client Response
15	(Couple's therapy) Lisa and Frank, let's suppose that our meeting together is helpful to you. How will you know that our time together has been useful?	*Lisa:* Definitely he would be talking about his feelings.
16	On a scale from 0 to 10, where 10 is the miracle, where would you put yourself?	Zero.
17	On a scale from 0 to 10, where 10 is the miracle, where would you put yourself?	I'm way below zero.
18	On a scale from 0 to 10, where 10 is the miracle, where would you put yourself?	Negative 25.
19	On a scale from 0 to 10, where 10 is the miracle, where would you put yourself?	Oh, right now? I'm at a 15!
20	Let's suppose that things went from just 2 to 3. How would you know?	I would be happy.
21	Let's suppose that things went from just 2 to 3. How would you know?	I really couldn't tell you about 3, but I could tell you about 10.
22	On a scale of 0 to 10, where 10 is that you have every confidence that things could get better and 0 is that you have little confidence, where would you put yourself?	I have no confidence that things could get better.
23	On a scale from 0 to 10, where 10 is the miracle, where would you put yourself?	How can you put a number on my problems?
24	On a scale from 0 to 10, where 10 is the miracle, where would you put yourself?	I have no idea.
25	Let's suppose that our meeting together is helpful to you. How will you know that our time together has been useful?	I'm glad you asked me. The space aliens would stop following me.

The therapist then must respond as if the client actually spoke the words. The conversation continues until the workshop leader perceives that the conversation has begun to move into a solution-building direction. The role-play can then be stopped and discussion, alternative interventions, and comments are encouraged. It is important for the workshop leader to support the therapist and compliment the therapist's efforts in order to create a sense of safety, spontaneity, and fun.

EXPERIENCE

When I first proposed the workshop for the SFBTA 2008 Annual Conference on Solution-Focused Practices, I imagined that we would easily go through all 25 scenarios within the hour and 15 minutes allotted for the workshop. Because of the lively discussions that followed each scenario, we were only able to get through about 3 of the 25 video examples, much to my amazement. We had one individual who had been chosen to be the therapist. She stated that she was new to solution focus but was willing to try. Using the workshop participants' suggestions, she was able to do a very credible job and deservingly received kudos from the group.

FINAL ADVICE

The advice is very simple: Keep it safe; compliment, compliment, compliment; and make it fun.

REFERENCE

Gilligan, S. (1987). *Therapeutic trances: The cooperation principle in Ericksonian hypnotherapy.* New York: Brunner/Mazel.

53

SEMAPHORE, METAPHOR,...TWO-BY-FOUR

Frank Thomas

Back in the early 1990s, I was finishing up a solution-focused (SF) supervision[1] training when one of the attendees asked me how I would handle supervisees who "just don't get it." He was skeptical of a supervisory approach that focused on strengths, abilities, and cooperation—with good reason: Working from a position of supervisor-as-expert was all he had ever known. His example: "I have a supervisee/therapist who won't take suggestions. If I believe he is practicing outside his expertise, misreading a situation, and so on, I try to offer my ideas in a way that isn't a directive. However, he doesn't seem to think any of my ideas will work so he ignores them. How can you work with someone who is resistant like this?"

There are limitations to any model or approach to supervision/training. When a supervisor assumes a nonexpert stance in a supervision relationship, she[2] knows that her knowledge and experience are still valuable assets. She simply begins with a similar mind-set each time she meets with a therapist[3] and each time she thinks about the relationship. This mind-set includes asking questions such as:

- How can I tread as softly as possible?
- What are my obligations and areas of influence?
- How do I meet my obligations (to the therapist, client, agency, licensure board, etc.) while keeping my nonexpert stance?
- How can I create freedom for the therapist while retaining the option of closing off therapist options when it is necessary to do so?

I've adopted an approach I call "semaphore, metaphor,...two-by-four" as a way of describing the process of moving from a generative, open-options position to a more restrictive, few-options stance with therapists in supervision.

SEMAPHORE

In the semaphore system of communication, square flags are attached to two short poles. The signaler indicates specific letters and numbers by holding the flags in various arm positions.[4] My father was a signalman in the U.S. Navy, so I grew up hearing stories about his use of Morse code and semaphore. When ships wanted to communicate without breaking radio silence, they used flag signals known as semaphore during the day and blinking Morse code light signals at night.

Semaphore is simple digital communication. To get the signal receiver's attention, person A waves the flags up and down on either side of the body and then begins signaling one letter at a time. Once the message is completed, the receiver (person B) sends a signal: "message received." There may or may not be a follow-up message, and how the message is received or understood by B is unknown until B replies.

In supervision, "semaphore" communication happens all the time, especially given the power difference between supervisor and therapist. Supervisors constantly give ideas, suggestions, opinions, and information; therapists tell supervisors, "Message received." Until therapists return to supervision, it is difficult to know how the messages are understood and/or implemented. This supervision lag time along with the ambiguity that usually accompanies suggestions can lead to wonderful therapist discoveries as well as varying understandings of what were suggestions and what might have been directives. Therapists supervised by SF supervisors hopefully hear these digital messages as, "Here is another option among several possible options, one of which is to continue what you have already been doing."

Semaphore: A Clinical Illustration

An illustration may help: Bob is a first-semester practicum student seeking a master's degree in counseling from the university. In his second career, Bob described his latest attempts to "help Rich and Maria get it" during the weekly supervision session. Susan, the supervisor, is a seasoned therapist and clinical trainer.

The couple came to see Bob because their pastor referred them to the university marriage and family therapy clinic for "communication problems." After three sessions, they had still not established a goal for therapy with Bob. Bob showed a portion of the third-session video that he believed illustrated his best attempts, but he was frustrated with the results.

Susan had several ideas about Bob's development of expertise with the SF approach and wanted to offer them as indirectly as possible. She believed curiosity about possibilities, exceptions, and past successes was her best general approach as an SF supervisor. She had been persistently curious about Bob's past successes in setting goals with other couples, but Bob's consistent response in this case was to ignore his past success and work harder to get what he believed must happen to happen.[5] She decided to adopt a somewhat more direct approach with Bob while staying solution focused, starting with a semaphore-like response:

Bob: They (Rich and Maria) just don't get it! They have to set a *goal!* (Bob rolls his eyes)

Susan: Some people just don't get it. Perhaps the "communication problems" that brought them to therapy in the first place are part of this goal-setting struggle. (The session moves on to other matters.)

Bob's internal conversation after supervision: I wonder if I've missed the connection between the presenting problem and what's problematic in the session. Have I become part of this problem? Why am I insisting they have a goal? If I don't have a customer relationship with them, pushing a goal would be inappropriate (a generative, self-reflexive time for Bob).

METAPHOR

When I speak of "metaphor" in this chapter, I am referring to relating stories that create space for interpretation and choice by the therapist. Well-crafted stories and metaphorical examples are more ambiguous than the semaphore messages because possible directives are even less obvious to the therapist. This can create exchanges in supervision like this:

Supervisor: That reminds me of a client I saw years ago…(a quick story).

Therapist: Are you telling me I should do what you did?

Supervisor: Oh no, it's simply a story that came to mind that I thought you might find interesting.

When the creative supervisor learns ways to offer ideas indirectly on a consistent basis, therapists usually stop asking the preceding question; they discover that the supervisor really is *not* trying to get a message/moral across and is simply adding requisite variety to the supervisory conversation. The ambiguity creates a different kind of space for therapists to consider alternatives the indirect touches areas of the unconscious that direct messages do not. When supervisory relationships allow for such ambiguity, which can create discomfort for some, "do something different" can become a reality.

Metaphor: A Clinical Illustration

Picking up the case again, we find that Bob has requested a supervision session with Susan to "bounce around some ideas" before his next session with Rich and Maria. He is familiar with Susan's storytelling and knows that her metaphors are not directives.

Bob: I've been thinking about the connections between Rich and Maria's presenting problem—they have difficulties coming to agreements on things—and what's happening with me in counseling. Boy, it's humbling! But I don't feel like I have a lot of options; it's not my first case with a couple, but I know I lack experience (an opening many supervisors take, giving advice or directives).

Susan: You know, I was talking to a colleague who told me about a therapist she supervised years ago. That therapist was very creative but he continually moved too quickly with his clients, often leaving them behind by forcing direction and pace on them. She told the therapist, "I admire your enthusiasm. It reminds me of a man who mashed the accelerator in his car every time he got lost. When passengers asked about this rapid acceleration, he always said, 'Well, I don't know where we are or where we're going, but we're making really good time!'"

Bob's postsession internal conversation: I can see Rich in that story—he's always rushing off and leaving Maria out of decisions that affect her. So, it makes sense that she would be digging in her heels, which might make Rich work even harder to set a goal Maria doesn't agree with...*or,* maybe it's *me* who's rushing off in directions Rich and Maria can't make sense of...*now* I have some options! I can ask them for their opinions on the pace and direction *or* simply tell them we need to "go slow"[6] *or* apologize to them because I now realize *I* have been part of this goal-setting struggle *or...* (Bob generates multiple options).

TWO-BY-FOUR

For those unfamiliar with the U.S. system of measurement, a two-by-four (shortcut: 2×4) is a piece of construction lumber of varying lengths—approximately 2 inches deep and 4 inches wide—that can be used as a club. This is a violent image, but for me it fits: The 2×4 method is the most controlling way to get both the therapist's attention and his cooperation. When training supervisors, I have found the "whack on the head with a 2×4" to be the most common stance taken when the supervisor assumes an expert position and gives directives to the therapist. I see this as therapy-once-removed; that is, the supervisor is actually conducting the therapy, using a form of ventriloquism to speak to the clients through a compliant therapist.

Because I value supervision that opens up possibilities for therapists, I would recommend that the 2×4 approach be used only when the clinical context demands supervisor control and other, less direct methods have failed. There are such moments, but SF supervisors make the 2×4 the last resort rather than the first.

Two-by-Four: Clinical Illustration

Continuing the saga of Bob and his supervisor Susan: Bob returns the following week to report that Rich and Maria have separated and will no longer be in marital therapy together. Rich called to tell Bob the news and asked that their complete clinical record be sent to his attorney, as he is seeking a divorce from Maria. Here is the supervisory exchange between Bob and Susan:

Bob: I've already made a copy of the file to give to Rich; after all, it *is* his file.
Susan: Bob, it's not his file; it's their file. State laws on confidentiality are very clear on what we can and cannot do with client files when two or more adults are involved in therapy.
Bob: But I think it's his right to have a copy of the file.
Susan: Well, it's not, and here's what we have to consider before any more communication takes place….This is what you cannot do….This is what you must do… (few options, greater supervisor control, very direct and unambiguous).

FINAL THOUGHTS

I've written extensively on solution-focused supervision (Thomas, 1996, 2000) and I am convinced that the main reason more supervisors do not experiment with the SF approach in supervision is because they feel they must leave other options behind. The workshop attendee's concerns that began this chapter are legitimate—there are limits with any therapy or supervision approach, and SF approaches are no different (Thomas, 2007). But, when necessary, a deliberate and gradual shift from most options to fewest options allows for supervisory flexibility, and adapting this semaphore–metaphor–2×4 approach may create possibilities for those new to a solution-focused, nonexpert stance in supervision. May the "phors" be with you!

NOTES

1. Thanks to Thorana Nelson, John Wheeler, and many of the therapists I've supervised for bouncing this idea around with me over the years. John's chapter (Wheeler, 2007) is recent and is one of the best articulations of a solution-focused supervisory approach.
2. In this chapter, supervisors will be females and therapists will be males to avoid confusion around pronouns.

3. To flatten the power difference a bit, I refer to supervisees and trainees as therapists throughout the chapter. They deserve the respect, and they've earned it.
4. Perhaps the most famous signal in this system is the peace symbol: a combination of the semaphoric letters N and D, standing for "nuclear disarmament."
5. This contradicts a maxim of SFT: If it doesn't work, don't do more of it—do something different.
6. A tip of the hat to John Weakland, a skilled grandparent of the SF model; grammatically, it should be "go slow*ly*."

REFERENCES

Thomas, F. N. (1996). Solution-focused supervision: The coaxing of expertise in training. In S. D. Miller, M. A. Hubble, & B. L. Duncan (Eds.), *Handbook of solution-focused brief therapy: Foundations, applications, and research* (pp. 128–151). San Francisco: Jossey–Bass.

Thomas, F. N. (2000). Mutual admiration: Fortifying your competency-based supervision experience. *RATKES: Journal of the Finnish Association for the Advancement of Solution and Resource Oriented Therapy and Methods, 2,* 30–39.

Thomas, F. N. (2007). Possible limitations, misunderstandings, and misuses of solution-focused brief therapy. In T. S. Nelson & F. N. Thomas (Eds.), *Handbook of solution-focused brief therapy: Clinical applications* (pp. 391–408). Binghamton, NY: Haworth.

Wheeler, J. (2007). Solution-focused supervision. In T. S. Nelson & F. N. Thomas (Eds.), *Handbook of solution-focused brief therapy: Clinical applications* (pp. 343–370). Binghamton, NY: Haworth.

54

CERTIFICATE OF COMPETENCE

John Wheeler

INTRODUCTION

The Certificate of Competence is a tool designed to help practitioners realise, recognise, and remember the abilities, values, and beliefs they bring to their work with clients. Readers will first be taken through the process of creating their own certificate. An account will then be given of why and how the tool was created. The chapter will conclude with examples of how the tool has been put to use and adapted to other circumstances.

THE CERTIFICATE

The certificate uses a series of seven questions and prompts (see Figure 54.1). Take your time. Sometimes answers arise quickly, sometimes it takes a while, and sometimes important surprises come about when you let your brain relax and search around a bit.

First Prompt

"When I do my work I take my inspiration from the following people…"

When you do the work you do, where do you take your inspiration from? You may bring to mind a person in a similar line of work, someone who was a good example of how to do your work well. You may recall someone you came across in training or through reading. You may recall a historical character. Some of your sources of inspiration may not be in your line of work at all; they may be a relative or friend.

Certificate of competence

For _____

Date _____

When I do my work I take my inspiration from the following people,

These people have taught me that when I do my work it is most important to remember the following,

These are the people who encouraged me to do the work I do,

Figure 54.1 The Certificate of Competence.

One person who trained as a nurse remembered that when she was a student on the wards she was particularly impressed by a qualified nurse who loved her work and was well liked by the patients. She remembered thinking at the time how much she wanted to be like her.

Another person knew that she had been significantly inspired by her father as she was growing up. She remembered in particular a time when she was very young. Her father had taken her into the garden and invited her to find two identical pansies. After a while she found she was unable to do so, at which point her father explained to her that

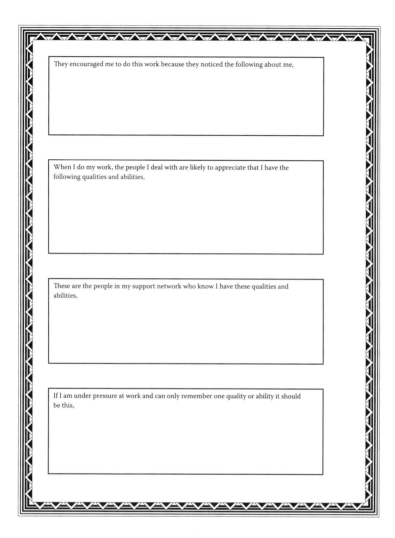

They encouraged me to do this work because they noticed the following about me,

When I do my work, the people I deal with are likely to appreciate that I have the following qualities and abilities,

These are the people in my support network who know I have these qualities and abilities,

If I am under pressure at work and can only remember one quality or ability it should be this,

Figure 54.1 (Continued) The Certificate of Competence.

they were all different from each other. He then went on to explain that it was the same with people too and he hoped she would always remember this. Remembering that everyone is unique has turned out to be very important in her work with children who have experienced domestic violence.

Second Prompt

"These people have taught me that when I do my work it is most important to remember the following..."

Again, take your time. Think of each person you have identified in response to the first question. Imagine each person being with you now, talking to you. What would each be likely to say?

Third Prompt

"These are the people who encouraged me to do the work I do…"

Who are the people who encouraged you to do the work you are doing? These may be friends or relatives who encouraged you to embark on your line of work in the first place. These may be people who taught you in early stages of your training. These may be people who managed you and recognised your potential.

One person recalled the encouragement of family members when she decided to embark upon professional training. She was the first in the family to do so. She could still recall people saying, "Go for it!" Another person recalled a manager saying, "You're wasted here. You should get yourself into some professional training."

Fourth Prompt

"They encouraged me to do this work because they noticed the following about me…"

Again, take your time. Put humbleness and embarrassment to one side. Trust their judgment. They must have noticed something about you; otherwise, they wouldn't have said what they said. What must they have been noticing about you? What could have prompted them to have said what they said? If it helps, imagine their being with you now and ask them.

Fifth Prompt

"When I do my work, the people I deal with are likely to appreciate that I have the following qualities and abilities…"

You might consider what users of your service, in general, appreciate. You may be able to recall specific comments made to you by clients you have worked with.

One practitioner looked back on a meeting where she had done her best to advocate for a young person in a meeting with other practitioners, but with no obvious effect on the outcome of the meeting. As she left the meeting, the parents of the young person commented that they didn't know how they would have coped with the meeting if she hadn't been there—a powerful endorsement of what she had contributed.

Sixth Prompt

"These are the people in my support network who know I have these qualities and abilities..."

These may be fellow practitioners or they may be friends or relatives.

If you want to hold on to your use of a second language, spending time with people you can use it with helps. In the same way, our values, beliefs and abilities are more likely to stay alive if we spend time with people who value them.

Sometimes the working environment can be hazardous to beliefs and values. Sometimes we find ourselves compromising our integrity. Sometimes this can happen to such an extent that we even become a different person, forgetting who we once were.

One practitioner found that his qualities were not being encouraged at work so he set up a group of like-minded people so he wouldn't lose himself.

Seventh Prompt

"If I am under pressure at work and can only remember one quality or ability it should be this..."

By now you have a rich description of yourself, drawing on your sources of inspiration, the people who have encouraged you, and what clients appreciate you for. Your answer to this question is likely to be firmly located in these descriptions of who you can be. The quality is likely to be something that comes quite easily to you. It is likely to be well connected to your values and beliefs, and it is likely to lead on to other attributes you have recognised in yourself. In times at work when you feel like you have lost your footing, it is likely that when you act in this particular way, the uniqueness of who you can be has a chance of coming back more fully into being.

Now that you've explored your replies to the questions and prompts, you may be interested to visit www.johnwheeler.co.uk, where you will find a downloadable copy of the certificate. The design has been created so that people can have the advantage of a foldable pocket-size version. Pocket size means that you can easily keep it with you. The foldability means that if you have time to remind yourself of your replies to all the questions, then you can read them in order. On the other hand, if you have no more than a couple of seconds and need to be reminded of your answer to the last prompt, you can sneak a look by lifting the cover toward you.

HOW AND WHY WAS THE CERTIFICATE
OF COMPETENCE CREATED?

The tool first came into being when I was supervising a social work student who preferred to continue working in a solution-focused way once she was qualified and needed a way to hold on to what she had learnt through her training (Wheeler & Greaves, 2005). We knew Yvonne would gain an embossed certificate at the end of her training. We knew also, however, that the content of the certificate would be the same for every student who passed the course. We realised that we wanted something that would much more specifically say why Yvonne had passed her course, why she had done the training in the first place, and what, exactly, it was that she was able to carry into this world of practice.

We also hoped for something a little more portable than a framed certificate. Whilst framed certificates tell clients that the professional in front them has professional credibility, we wanted something that Yvonne could have a quiet look at to remind herself that she had professional credibility. We then asked ourselves to suppose that we had something like this: What would it look like? What would the categories of information be that might be useful to remember in the future? What were the questions and prompts that might elicit this information in a manner that was unique to Yvonne? And so the Certificate of Competence was created, along with a few refinements over time as the tool has been used with others and presented in workshops.

OTHER USES

Since creating the tool with Yvonne, I have put the certificate to a variety of uses and have heard of further uses that occurred to people who came across the tool in workshops.

Supervision

As a supervisor, I often use the Certificate of Competence at the beginning of a period of supervision. Supervisees have reported that the format provides them with a platform for letting me know a lot of relevant information very quickly. Knowing who has helped to construct the supervisee's professional identity gives me the opportunity to refer back to them in subsequent supervision conversations. "You feel quite stuck at the moment. If Bob, who recognised your professional potential, were here now, what do you think he'd suggest?" Knowing the values and beliefs the supervisees bring to their work and those who know they have them gives me the opportunity to ask questions such as, "As you try to maintain open-mindedness in your work with this client, what do you think that other client was noticing about you when she thanked you for being open-minded in your work with her?"

Job Interviews

Interviewees often worry that they will not give proper credit to themselves when being interviewed. Interviewers typically hope that the interview will help them know who the interviewee is so they can decide how well that person will fit the job requirements. Going through the Certificate of Competence has given people a chance to have a more comfortable understanding of who they are and what they bring to their work. The portability of the tool allows for a sneak review if necessary. A reminder of the other people who got them as far as they have already got in their work so far can be particularly helpful. Knowing you have your supporters with you in your head can make a big difference to how you feel.

Recharging Batteries

A group of practitioners and managers from a variety of settings attended a day designed to help them "recharge their batteries." The day included mindfulness exercises and exercises based on the solution-focused approach with the Certificate of Competence as a centrepiece of the day. People worked in pairs sharing their responses to the questions and prompts. Participants reported that the day greatly helped them to refocus and increased the energy and motivation they could put into their work.

Team Building

A management consultant used the tool with two sections of an organisation that used to be separate but now needed to get to know each other. Through the course of a team-building event, people paired up to share their replies, changing the pairing each time they were presented with a new question. Participants reported that this helped to forge significant new relationships very quickly

Back to Therapy

When I was working with a parent with very low self-esteem, I found the questions could be easily made appropriate for the situation she found herself in—for example,

- When you are being a mother to your children, where do you take your inspiration from?
- When I am being a parent, my children are likely to appreciate that I have the following qualities and abilities...
- If I am under pressure with my children and can only remember one quality or ability it should be this...

Other practitioners who have come across the certificate through workshops have imagined many other possible adaptations for use with the clients they work with. So, having seen what the Certificate of Competence is and seen other uses, what uses occur to you? In the event of your finding other uses not described here, please let me know.

REFERENCE

Wheeler, J., & Greaves, Y. (2005) Solution-focused practice teaching in social work. In T. S. Nelson (Ed.), *Education and training in solution-focused brief therapy* (pp. 177–187). New York: Haworth.

55

TOOLBOX FOR WORK-LIFE BALANCE

Brenda Zalter

- Pencil—reminds you to list your blessings and priorities every day.
- Eraser—reminds you that everyone makes mistakes and that is OK when we make an effort to learn from them, forgive ourselves, and move on.
- Hammer—reminds you not to hammer your ideas into others, but be fair and firm in your resolve and kind in your treatment of staff and clients alike.
- Level—reminds you to have a healthy balance between work, family, and friends.
- Measuring tape—reminds you that things don't always measure up but you have the ability to adjust because there is always plan B.
- Duct tape—reminds you to stick with it and you will be able to fix anything.

III
Theory

56

SOLUTION-FOCUSED BRIEF THERAPY AND WATERCOLOURS?

Paul Avard

Some time ago, I read a post on one of the solution-focused e-mail lists I subscribe to. A fellow practitioner had learned a new skill—I forget precisely what—and in describing it added that this new skill could be placed in her paint box and could be used with all the other colours to enhance her practice as necessary. This struck me as a lovely idea.

I thought about this and realised that, in terms of my own practice, adding colours to my paint box might be counterproductive! Why? As a watercolourist, I was taught that less is more. My watercolour teacher said that if she ever caught me using leaf green or sap green or some such other colour, she would do unspeakable things to me. She explained it as follows:

> Green and almost all other colours (primary colours excepted) are a combination of two, possibly three primary colours. The colours may be complementary or opposite, whichever you wish; however, what becomes obvious is that combining too many colours produces mud. And mud is opaque and acts in opposition to one of the finest qualities many watercolours have, which is translucence: The colour of the paper or the wash colour below the top colour shines through.
>
> In essence, if I can make green by using, for instance, cadmium yellow and cerulean (blue), then I will have a soft, gentle, and warm green and it shows. If I want a slightly more acidy green,

237

I will use lemon yellow and ultramarine. To darken my green, I might use alizarin crimson or another shade of red. Using these few colours not only preserves the qualities of light I'm looking for, but also ensures that what is underneath can shine through and reduces the number of colours I have to have in my paint box since I can combine the few colours I have in many, many ways— to good effect.

For me, my art is akin to my practice of solution-focused brief therapy: Use the least you need to enable the stories to shine through without muddying the paper; carry the smallest palette feasible. You will think harder to make sure you capture what is necessary, so, why not?

And now I'm moving toward monochrome pen work—black ink or sepia? That depends, but the few lines I use provide all the light, shade, and tone we need. The story is there, just look.

57

NEUROSCIENCE AND SOLUTION-FOCUSED BRIEF THERAPY

Or How SFBT Can Change the Brain

Phillip B. Ziegler

When my wife, Tobey Hiller, and I wrote our book, *Recreating Partnership: A Solution-Oriented, Collaborative Approach to Couples Therapy,* we were primarily influenced by our more than 50 combined years as practicing marital therapists and by ideas and practices associated with constructionist philosophy and solution-focused clinical practices derived from the work of Steve de Shazer and Insoo Kim Berg. From her clinical experience (not to mention our own marriage of more than 30 years at that time), Tobey formulated a clinically useful concept that supplemented solution-focused brief therapy (SFBT) and that was especially helpful when working with couples. We came to call this concept the "Good Story/Bad Story Narrative Continuum."

As Tobey explained it (she is, after all, a novelist as well as a clinician), partners in long-term relationships inevitably develop varying positive and negative stories about each other and their relationship. Naturally, in the honeymoon phase, the stories are mostly romantic and idealized and organized on the Good Story end of the narrative continuum. As the lovers view each other through the lens of this narrative, they see mainly positive qualities and interpret each other's gestures and conversations as proof that theirs is a relationship "made in heaven."

Over time, as we all too well know, the stories become more varied— falling more and more along both sides of this narrative continuum.

Irritating characteristics and displeasing actions by one's partner fall on the Bad Story side while pleasing ones continue to fall on the Good Story side. So long as the Good Story remains energetic and controlling, Bad Story pieces are viewed as isolated and lack the power to shape ongoing perception. But when, over time, the Bad Story narrative begins to thicken and compete with one or both partners' Good Stories, the relationship starts to enter a trouble zone.

If the Good Story is not rejuvenated and reinvigorated, and if the Bad Story continues to gain perceptual weight and influence each partner's view of the other, the relationship spirals downward *even if the partners try to change their behaviors*.[1] By the time the couple seeks professional help, both partners' Bad Story narratives have clouded over whatever traces of their Good Stories might still exist. And, even when the partners try to take steps to turn things around, the perceptual power of the Bad Story beclouds these efforts and things just get worse.

All too often, marital therapists (who might be highly skilled in individual therapy) and even many who are well versed in SFBT find themselves unable to alter the course of a couple's endless conversation that simply reinforces each partner's Bad Story. In consulting and supervision, we have been amazed how often we notice missed opportunities on the part of the therapist to co-construct "exceptions" or experiential bits and pieces of the imagined "miracle" pictures. Instead, the therapist slips into refocusing the conversation on problems, conflicts, and difficulties.

We wrote *Recreating Partnership* in 2000. We explained our own evolution away from problem focusing and communication skill building with couples toward a more solution-focused approach. In this approach, we oriented conversations around desired future pictures using the miracle question (Miller & Berg, 1995) and other questions that invite partners to envision and articulate observable happenings that reflect that desired future; "exceptions," when some of those desired happenings recently happened; and scaling to help partners identify small changes that could be made significant through further exploratory conversation. Our intention, whatever solution-focused inquiry we were using, was to engage the partners in conversations that could soften the power of their individual Bad Stories and invigorate their individual and shared Good Stories.

In the intervening years, we've not had the wish that we had written the book with ink that faded away. The ideas have continued to hold up for us and, from the feedback we get from therapists we've trained, supervised, and consulted with, they continue to be useful to them as well as they engage in the challenging and often confusing work of marital and couple therapy. We still feel that we pretty much said all we had to say about how we've integrated SFBT into our approach to couples therapy. So, why this chapter now?

What has stimulated this chapter is my reading in the field of neuroscience and mindfulness meditation, as well as my personal practice of the latter. I have been learning about some interesting and confirming research regarding how the brain, nervous system, and mind work in concert to shape our ongoing experience of ourselves, others, and the world around us. For example, Gazzaniga (2000) found that the narrative function takes place in the left prefrontal cortex. So, although the left hemisphere has been associated with language, logic, and literal processing of data, it also appears to be the source of our natural impulse to turn events into stories.

At the same time, the right hemisphere seems to be the site of compassionate and caring feelings and impulses. Several researchers, especially those studying mindfulness meditation and its effect on brain structure and functioning, suggest that when the storying function shifts from the left to the right hemisphere, people become more caring and compassionate, and less irritable, hostile, and depressed. Could this explain why SFBT and *Recreating Partnership* couples therapy seem to be so effective and efficient? Could it be that Good Story conversations—about miracle pictures, exceptions, and positive movement along change scales—decrease story generation from the left hemisphere while triggering activity in the right hemisphere?

Neuroscientist and clinician Dr. Daniel Siegel argues that mindfulness meditation, by decreasing activity of the left hemisphere in favor of the right, actually increases neural patterns and structures in the right hemisphere. He says, "Long before words, our brains are creating nonverbal narratives, assemblies of selected neural network firing patterns that then serve to order our sense of the world. Even perception at its most fundamental level is an assembled process" (2007, p. 143). He argues that the kinds of narratives we create actually alter what we notice, how we story events, AND produce observable changes in the physical nature of the brain.

It seems that cutting-edge neuroscience is providing a scientific basis for constructionist and constructivist philosophy: We create our world in our brains—or, as the Buddhists would say, "The world and our minds are one and the same." Reading the work of people like Dan Siegel, I am excited to think that not only do the stories we tell ourselves and others influence our perceptions, memories, and fantasies of the future, but they also affect the structures and functioning of the brain.

So although it has been my clinical and personal experience that thickening the Good Story narrative alters the way partners view each other and their relationship and that this changing view influences how they treat each other in relationship-enhancing ways, I am discovering that the kinds of conversations that take place during the clinical hour can alter how the partners' brains function and even possibly alter the structures of their brains. This could explain why seemingly casual, light, and superficial conversations about what's going well in the couple's relationship—often after only a handful of sessions—can profoundly alter the way the partners view each other and how they behave toward each other, creating an upward spiral of viewing and doing. To paraphrase the Buddhists, a marriage-story and a marriage are the same.

NOTE

1. For example, research indicates that in troubled relationships, people make more reparative gestures than in satisfying relationships. However, these gestures are not noticed and/or are not reciprocated and this failure of reparative gestures to get a positive response is in itself predictive of marital failure. See Gottman (1999).

REFERENCES

Gazzaniga, M. S. (2000). Cerebral specialization and interhemispheric communication: Does the corpus callosum enable the human condition? *Brain 123*, 1293–1326.

Gottman, J. M. (1999). *The marriage clinic: A scientifically based marital therapy.* New York: Norton.

Miller, S. D., & Berg, I. K. (1995). *The miracle method: A radically new approach to problem drinking.* New York: W. W. Norton.

Siegel, D. (2007). *The mindful brain.* New York: Norton.

Ziegler, P., & Hiller, T. (2001). *Recreating partnership: A solution-oriented, collaborative approach to couples therapy.* New York: Norton.

58

CHANGE WE CAN BELIEVE IN

Paolo Terni

Philosophy [and coaching] is a battle against the bewitchment of our intelligence by means of our *language*.

—Wittgenstein (1958), #109

After getting his authorization and changing a few details to protect my client's privacy, here goes: After the initial banter, I asked the client what he would like to work on. He stated that his problem was that he was not able to say "no." According to protocol, I inquired about what he wanted instead and what would be different then for him if he learned to say no to people. In reply, the client started telling his own story: He was a self-made man, an entrepreneur, and a local politician. He told his story with pride. It seemed clear that he had no problem being assertive or saying no. His narrative had epic tones.

So here is the first lesson I was reminded of: The "*problem*" is often a *belief* that has been formed by a process of *generalization, deletion,* and/or *distortion*. What fascinated me again and again was the richness of the world that is hidden behind such blanket statements offered by clients.

I followed up with the proper questions and the "problem" transformed itself into just a part of a complex puzzle of relationships, situations, and interactions in the life of the coachee. It felt like seeing a black-and-white snapshot first becoming a color picture, then becoming a clip, then a movie, with the camera rolling from different spots, offering different views and perspectives. My friend Peter Szabó has a nice metaphor for this: It is like tapping somebody on the shoulder and saying: "*I see it [the problem]. And look at what is there [pointing in another direction, then another, then another]!*"

The client started to see that he could say no and he could do that very forcefully, too! However, he believed he could not say no to his managers because then they would "leave." By finding exceptions and following up on those, the *frame expanded* (as my friend Robert Dilts would say); it is not a one-shot interaction! The managers' requests were embedded in a web of interactions where there were, as the client started to see, many signs of loyalty on their parts. The client got to the idea that he could say no to some requests, explaining why in the context of a conversation where other positive things are highlighted. He could say "yes," and he could say "no," and he could say "maybe," and he could laugh and he could ask questions.

To get to that idea, the client had to battle the "problem frame" that was kept alive by his own choice of words: "It is because I am afraid of loss"; "I have always been like that, even as a child"; "In my family…"—the past, the personality, the theories. *All bewitchment of our intelligence by means of our language.* It is as if everything else disappears—all the good things, all the achievements—and the problem becomes a huge idol that dominates the landscape of the client's perceptions, as if the client is hypnotized by this problem. I, the coach, can feel the pressure to solve the problem. Like a vortex that sucks attention and energies: "I can't say no"—the mantra, the belief. Quick, quick, let's solve it, let's dig deeper, let's be enchanted by complexity and emotions and history!

The client told me he had undergone psychoanalysis. I was impressed by how well he had learned that language game. He elaborated on his difficulties about accepting "loss." He talked about "mourning" and "transference." He tried again and again to bait me: He mentioned his family dynamics, his childhood, and how his company was like his family and he was "spoiling" his employees.

I said that he tried to bait me because every time he mentioned something like that, he would stare at the ground. Then he would sneak a peek at me, to see my reactions. I responded following protocol: I complimented him on his level of introspection; I invited him to build on that by asking about behaviors, third-party observations, and actual conversations while keeping everything in the present. I am sure that a practitioner of a different school would have followed up on that—on "the cause." I am sure there was a world to be discovered (or created?) there. Had I followed a neurolinguistic programming strategy (e.g., Bandler & Grinder, 1982), I would have worked on the client's belief—perhaps on how to change it using *sleight of mouth techniques* (Dilts, 1999). I stayed true to a solution-focused approach.

Within a solution-focused conversation, the client came up with a brilliant idea. He now knew that he knew how to say no. He was now able to consider different scenarios because he was in a positive mood, seeing his abilities, and being complimented all the time. He also saw that people did not leave him if he said no and that a request is part of a web of interactions and a specific context. Exploring exceptions, he now saw that he was able to say no effectively and convincingly when his "businessman" identity was triggered, when the conversation was focused on performance indicators and cost-effectiveness analyses and business strategies.

So, here was *his solution:* Create a procedure for authorizing new benefits, incentives, pay raises, or changes in the allocation of projects. The procedure included filling out a form; it included a holding period and each request had to be audited by the CFO. This was quite a change for someone used to rewarding his employees on the spot; that is, it was quite a change from over-relying on instincts and bowing to requests based on fear rather than on business sense! Still, a simple solution.

We did not need to "dig deep" and talk about the past, about the unconscious, about projections, about family dynamics, about the fear of loss and of death. We did not need to find the "cause" in the psyche. We did not develop the generalization, "I can't say no" into a theory of personality, a trait of the client, or a fact he had to explain and deal with. We stayed on the surface.

We deconstructed the generalization, "I can't say no": What happens when you say no? What is different? What else? What do you say? What do others say? Where? When?

> What we do is to bring words back from their metaphysical to their everyday use.

> **—Wittgenstein (1958), #116**

REFERENCES

Bandler, R., & Grinder, J. (1982). *Reframing: Neuro-linguistic programming and the transformation of meaning.* Moab, UT: Real People Press.

Dilts, R. (1999). *Sleight of mouth: The magic of conversational belief change.* Capitola, CA: Meta Publications.

Wittgenstein, L. (1958). *Philosophical investigations* (3rd ed.). New York: Macmillan.

IV

Stories, Poems, Songs, and Solution-Focused Quotes

59

FRIDAY NIGHT SERVICE

Harriet E. Kiviat

September, 2004

Shabbat Shalom. Some of you who have seen me here on holidays and special occasions or have met me before probably know me as "the cantor's mother." I would like to thank "my daughter, the cantor" and Rabbi Potasnik for asking me to speak to you tonight about starting anew.

Let me tell you a little more about why I have been asked to speak to you. My name is Harriet Kiviat, I am a professional counselor, and I live and work in West Hartford, Connecticut. I spent the first 22 years of my life in Brooklyn before migrating to Staten Island and eventually up yonder to Connecticut. I hold a master's degree in community counseling with a specialization in child welfare and am awaiting the confirmation of my Connecticut licensure and national certification. My work is primarily with adolescents and their families and I specialize in working with people who have been abused. Most of the therapeutic work that I do is based on the theory that everyone, no matter what his or her problem, has strengths. I work with my clients cooperatively and together we identify these strengths within them to set goals for going forward.

This evening as we congregate after 2 days of intensive praying, I invite you to relax, listen, absorb, and contemplate. I will be asking you to think about things. You don't have to work hard tonight, though you can if you choose to. It's all about choice—your choice—and I hope that when you leave here you will have a new perspective for the coming year.

Starting anew...this is an appropriate topic at this time of year. We are given a gift each year at Rosh Hashanah; we are offered the chance of new beginnings, we are given the opportunity to cast away our sins, and we acknowledge the possibility that change will occur in the coming year. As long as we are alive, the one thing that we can be sure of is that nothing *ever* stays the same.

So, when change does come—and it can be good or bad—how do we prepare for the alterations in our lives? How do we deal with the repercussions of these changes? How do we take control of the things that *are* in our power? How do we turn pain and suffering into blessings?

How many times do you listen to the rabbi's sermons, hearing his inspirational words, nodding your head in agreement, and leaving the synagogue with all intentions of making a change or doing something different? Nevertheless, how many times have you actually taken the opportunity to make changes...to think about what would be different if you dared to veer off of your predetermined course? Am I going to tell you anything new today? No, I don't think so, but, perhaps, you'll hear it differently.

Now, I would like to ask you all a different kind of question. This question has no right or wrong answer and requires some imagination on your part. When I am finished asking this question, I encourage you to think about how you would answer.

> I invite you to relax now, close your eyes if you wish and let your imagination run free. Suppose, when this evening's services are concluded, we share a few words with each other...perhaps a little nosh...and then you go home. And after you are home you do whatever you do before you turn in for the night...maybe think a little about your experiences of the past few days. Then you go to sleep and, while you are sleeping, a miracle happens! And the miracle is that all of the problems that you are faced with today, big or small—anything that is getting in your way or causing you concern—all of these problems are gone...disappeared...like that (snap)!!! Only, you don't know that this miracle has happened because you are asleep. When you wake up in the morning, how will you know that a miracle happened? What will be the first thing that you will notice that will make you aware that this has occurred? If you can't notice this miracle, how will your significant other, or your parent, or your child know? What will they say is different?

Now, I have no way of knowing what your miracle is, but perhaps you are thinking, "I would feel that a weight has been lifted off my shoulders," or "I would not be in pain," or "My illness will be gone," or "I will have a special person sleeping in bed next to me," or "My mother wouldn't be yelling at me to clean my room," or "I will be going to work at a job that I love." There is no right or wrong answer; each one of you is different, so your miracle is different.

Now, let's take this one step further and think about this. What will you be doing differently when your miracle happens? What one thing can you think of that you are not doing now? One of my teenaged clients, just last week, came to me and said, "Remember that miracle we talked about—that my mother would be like acting like a real mom? Well, the weird thing is that it's starting to happen…she's being a little nice to me."

"Oh really," I said. "And what are you doing differently now that you weren't doing before?"

"Well" she replied, "I can be nice back to her a little…and…I am not scared to wake up anymore."

What if you are thinking, "There is no such thing as a miracle. My circumstances cannot change and I am not in control of what happens to me"? Okay, let's talk about that. Perhaps you are thinking, "My loved one would still be alive. That would be my miracle and I know that that can't happen." Well, you would be right. Unfortunately, there are things that happen to us—occurrences that impact our lives—that cannot be changed. However, it is up to you to decide how you want your future to unfold despite what has come to pass.

I'd like to share a story about a woman who did not believe that miracles could happen. I heard this story at a workshop last March. Speaker Bill O'Hanlon, a professional counselor and marriage and family therapist, told of the renowned psychologist Dr. Sol Gordon, who had been counseling a woman for many years around issues of abuse. The woman showed no signs of improvement and Dr. Gordon was at a loss of how to help her. He informed his client that he could no longer see her since the therapy that he was doing with her seemed not to help after so many years. She did not trust anyone and saw no way that she could ever establish and maintain any kind of relationship. Because of the abuse that she had endured, she had no self-esteem or feelings of self-worth.

As a last ditch effort to get the woman to take some steps forward, he prescribed "mitzvah therapy." Dr. Gordon believes that changes in your life can come merely by doing a small good deed—through the act of doing a mitzvah. He suggested to this woman that she go to a local treatment center for children who had been abused and offer to volunteer there. She maintained that she had nothing to offer. Dr. Gordon told her that this was her only option if she wanted to improve her life.

The woman hesitantly showed up at the treatment center and offered to volunteer. She talked to the children, played games with them, and within a short time, they started to look forward to her visits and she started to look forward to going to the center. The children would run to her and hug her when she walked in. All of this was very new for this woman, who had spent much of her life feeling worthless and ashamed. During this same time, she started to notice another worker at the center—a man. He was not very good looking, but she saw his heart shine through in the work that he did with the children. Apparently, he saw the same in her because they started dating and eventually got into a loving relationship.

Did this woman see miracles in her future? No, not at all. Was she able to make a change? Absolutely—but, she needed a little push in the right direction…and that's OK too.

So, now ask yourself, "What do I have to offer? What about me am I proud of, what do I think I do well?" And go out there and share it with someone. Better yet, do you have an experience that you could share that would let someone else know that they are not alone?

I have another story for you. This one is about a woman who, 13 years ago, was diagnosed with the neuromuscular disorder myasthenia gravis. She had difficulty breathing, speaking, and walking, and could barely see through her half-closed eyes. The doctors were not very optimistic for her future as it took so long to diagnose the illness and the medical treatment included heavy doses of medications and invasive surgery. The doctors told her that in 10 years time she would probably be in a wheelchair. At the same time, this woman had a family to raise. Her children were all in their teens, and this was not the time to get an illness like this.

Needless to say, she was not always a pleasure to live with and there was a lot of strain put on everyone in her support system to cope with this debilitating disease. Anyway, she did whatever she could to stay involved in the community and in her children's lives. In time, she came to see this illness as a blessing: She could not work, so she was always around to give emotional support to everyone. She also started volunteering some time at the local Jewish community center and found herself producing, directing, and costuming in excess of a dozen theatrical performances in which children ages 9 to 18 (including her own children) participated.

After this almost 5-year stint and finding herself an empty nester, she started to feel useless again and attempted to go back to work in the corporate world. However, the schedule and the regimen were too physically taxing. Besides, as she tells it, she missed hanging with all the kids!

A rehabilitation specialist took notice of her and observed that what this woman loved to do was work with teenagers. "You should be a counselor," she said.

The woman laughed and said, "Yeah, right. That would mean going to school again. How would I do that?"

"You have it within you to do whatever you want. Follow your bliss."

That conversation took place in April of 1999. Oh…you want to know what happened? Well, that woman is standing before you tonight telling you that you, too, can start anew.

I would like to challenge you: Next time we meet, let me know just how many times your miracle occurred—if only for a fleeting moment. Moreover, when that miracle occurred, what did you notice that was different? What else changed because you took a chance? When we recite the Shehechianu, we thank G-d for bringing us to this season, so let us take this one step further; let us receive this gift, take charge, and allow G-d to guide us as we go beyond this season… into our future. Rabbi Naomi Levy suggests in her writing that it is a blessing to compose one's own personal prayers as a supplement to one's communication with G-d. At this time, in keeping with the idea of doing something different, I invite you all to compose your own prayer silently, or you may share in the one that I have written for tonight:

> G-d, please give us the strength to open our hearts and minds to the possibility of miracles. Please give us the strength to walk the path that enables us to turn our pain into blessings. Allow us to understand that change is inevitable. G-d, please stand beside us as we choose to do something different. Amen. Shabbat Shalom.

60

MICHELANGELO'S SECRET WEAPON

Carole Waskett

It's a little known fact that BRIEF, that esteemed solution-focused training centre in London, has had a long and well-travelled history. One of its earliest gigs took it to Florence in the autumn of the first year of the sixteenth century. And there, amongst an enthusiastic local audience, was one Michelangelo, an artist. Actually, he'd made a bit of a mistake. He needed a break from art. The endless crashing and banging of sculpting had made him a bit deaf. He was getting rather sick of pasta and thought he'd signed up for a course in "beef cookery" rather than "brief therapy." But anyhow, he had ended up in the middle of a row so it was a bit tricky to get out. And the bloke seemed quite interesting, even if, to the artist's eye, his PowerPoint was crap.

The following September, the 26-year-old started work on the huge block of stone. For some reason, that solution-focused course kept coming back to his mind. The artist had been envisaging his preferred future for some time, describing, drawing, and almost feeling the sublime figure that he knew resided in the marble. He was driving his mates mad with it down the tavern. They said he was so distracted that he—ahem—"forgot" to buy his round most nights. Now he looked at his rough, strong, and capable hands, and knew that his passion, training, and ability would carry him through this great project; he had the strengths and resources to do it.

As the months went by, the artist's confidence grew. A year in, he scaled his efforts: Where 10 meant that he was on track, how was he doing? The work was hard, but the figure was emerging from the marble; he gave himself a 7. Late that night over a cocoa, he talked it through with his mum. "Yep, 7 would be about it," he said (in Italian). "How come?" asked his mum (also in Italian). Well, by affirming and appreciating their finer qualities, he'd got those blasted labourers to remove the spare lumps of marble from the workshop, and the bum was beginning to look like a proper bum at last. Michelangelo knew a good bum when he saw it, and this one had to be just perfect.

"What would be happening when he was at an 8?" Mum asked as she washed up the cups. She was a fast learner; she'd made the tea at that course and had been leaning against a pillar watching from the back.

"All right, all right," her son said rather grumpily; his shoulders were hurting. "So let's dream...an 8? Get those muscles right in the arms: Poor bloke's never going to beat Goliath without some decent biceps. Maybe this time next year...." In the morning he'd go for that next little concrete—well, marble—step: The cuticle on that left little finger could do with a seeing to. And...he drifted off to sleep before his mum could give him a tea towel.

Another September, 1504: the great unveiling. Michelangelo, battered but proud, took his accolades as his *David* towered above him. He knew deep in his bones that solution-focused thinking had got him through. And what was the next little step in his career? Somebody had mentioned something about doing a few frescoes in the Sistine Chapel. With his new psychological tool, it would be a piece of cake.

61

CREATING CALM OUT OF CHAOS

Using Solution-Focused Techniques With Family Members[1]

Harriet E. Kiviat

Solution-focused therapy is such an integral part of my life that my husband can be heard asking me, "And after you wake up, how will you know the miracle happened? What will you notice is different?" I don't question *his* use of the miracle question (Berg & Miller, 1992; De Jong & Berg, 1998; de Shazer, 1988), but if I were to ask the same question of him, my intent might be called into question.

As therapists, we often have mixed feelings about using our professional knowledge in our personal lives. Oftentimes, we are called upon by family members to "help" them with their problems, only to be told, "I want you to be my mother [friend, wife, etc.], not my therapist!" So, what are we to do? We cannot ignore all that we know; how do we use our skills wisely in our own day-to-day interactions with our loved ones without taking the risks of crossing the boundaries?

Back in 2000, about 1 year into my studies in my master's program, I had the opportunity to travel to Milwaukee for one of Insoo and Steve's solution-focused therapy workshops. I was the only student among the group of practicing clinicians and educators. At the time, I was struggling with how all of my new knowledge translated into my daily life. Just a short time prior to that, my dad had been ill and he had been experiencing some stress and anxiety over medical procedures. I found myself using some "therapeutic techniques" to help him relax, but I was plagued with the concern that it was not appropriate for me to do so. Serendipitously, I found myself in a conversation with Insoo and I asked her opinion on that subject. In her inimitable way, she looked at me and said, "Ahhh…did that work for your dad?" I responded affirmatively; she stopped for a brief moment and said, "Then if it works, do more of it!"

In this chapter, I show how scaling, compliments, recognizing what works, and the miracle question—all techniques that I first learned that weekend from Insoo and Steve—have enabled me to help my own family members create solutions in their own lives.

INTRODUCTION TO INTERVENTION

My 7½-year-old grandson is autistic. He is a beautiful boy with the soul of an angel, but the nature of the condition causes life in his household to be unpredictable and often chaotic. His energetic and delightful 5½-year-old sister adds her own special touch to this vibrant family of four. My daughter works full-time and my son-in-law is a stay-at-home dad who spends much of his time making sure that my grandson eats the right foods and gets to his therapies on time. Both parents shuttle the kids to extracurricular programs and ensure that the family has plenty of special time together.

One morning when they were visiting, I happened to be sitting with them at the kitchen table when they asked how I would help a client who came in with similar problems to theirs. I asked for clarification, thinking that they were going to ask about living with an autistic child. They declared that their life was "chaotic." I delicately asked if they were asking for help and they said yes. The following is a short version of the simple intervention that I implemented with my children (D = my daughter, S = my son-in-law, B = my grandson, G = my granddaughter):

What Are You Doing That Already Works?

Me: So, if I were at your place tomorrow morning, what would I notice that you are already doing that helps keep the chaos to a minimum?

S: I make the kids breakfast and their lunches so that D can get ready for work.

Me: And is that working?

They both agree that it works, but proceed to come up with the idea that if they were able to make the lunches the night before, it could ease things in the morning. By inquiring as to what they are already doing well, they came up with something to make things even better.

What Do You Know Does Not Work?

Me: I'm not living with you, and I would be the last person to judge what it is like living in your house. Would you mind at all sharing with me something that you know does not work for you guys?

D: Well, for me it's not having time to eat. I'm always in a rush. I would love to have the time to make a shake for breakfast the way you do and be able to have my lunch made to take to work. I even got a refrigerator for my office, but I never have time to make anything to put in it!

From this point, they were able to determine that if the ingredients for the shake were in the house, S could prepare the shake for both of them while he was preparing breakfast for the kids.

Compliments

Me: You know something? When I am with you, I marvel at how you guys handle everything on your plates. I wonder if you realize what a great job you are doing.

They may have been surprised to hear the words that way because it was different from simply saying, "I am proud of you." This gave them the opportunity to give themselves credit for their great work.

Scaling the Level of Chaos and the Miracle Question

Me: On a scale of 1 to 10, where 1 is the most chaotic and 10 is, "Ahhhhh…things are so calm…"

Both: Yeah, like that will ever happen!

Me: Oh…just humor me a little [they smile]…where were you on that scale before you left the house to come over today?

D: I'd say about a 3. It was nuts!

(Instead of going forward and finding out what it would take to get to a 3.5, I decided to attempt the miracle question. I made sure that I couched it appropriately and very lightheartedly.)

Me: Have you heard me talk about the miracle question?

D: Yeah…that's what we need: a miracle [giggles all around].

Me: OK…you might think this is very silly, but can I ask anyway?

Both: Sure.

Me: So, suppose after you get home this evening and after you do whatever you need to tonight, you go to bed…

D: OH NO! You're not going there, Mom, are you???? [we all have a good laugh at the innuendo]

Me: Nooooo…you go to SLEEP [they smile] and, while you are asleep, a miracle happens and the miracle is that the chaos has disappeared [snap] just like that! Only you don't know that it happened because you have been sleeping. What will be the first thing that you will notice when you wake up that will let you know that the miracle has happened?

D: The organization chart that I got for the kids would be hanging on the wall and they would know exactly what they had to do so we wouldn't have to fight with them to get ready.

(I noted that D and S have already started to think of ways to make life easier for themselves.)

Level of Chaos on the Scale the Day After the Miracle

D: Oh…at least an 8.

S: Yeah!

This was an easy step for them to visualize; they were already doing many things that could lead them toward their miracle.

Scaling Level of Confidence

Me: OK, just one more time…

D: On a scale of 1 to 10…

Me: Ha, ha, ha! You want to finish? [the humor was so important]

D: No, go ahead [smiling]

Me: How confident are you that you could start implementing something that we talked about?

S: Oh…I am going to the grocery when we get home so I can get the stuff for the shakes, so I would say an 8 or 9.

Me: That's awesome. Let me know how the shakes taste!

Sometimes, it is just a matter of helping to refocus, and who better to do that than a mom!

In this case, please keep in mind that D and S never know what is going to happen with B; all good intentions can fly right out the window if he has a meltdown. Additionally, G has needs that have to be attended to. However, one of the most important things to consider when involving yourself with your family members is to keep it simple and to the point. I found that I had to keep checking myself to make certain that I was not "doing therapy." I watched and listened carefully and respectfully and made sure that humor was a large part of our time together.

It was apparent that they were seriously considering the task. I kept reminding them (and myself) that baby steps are very important; they shouldn't think that because we were coming up with all these ideas that they had to run out and do everything. A few days later, they did report that they had implemented one thing and it had made a difference. A few weeks later, my son-in-law called, asking me to remind him of something that we had discussed, therefore indicating that the ideas remained with them. It was a great experience all around.

A NOTE OF CAUTION

Marriage and family therapists have to make a conscientious effort not to engage in dual roles within their purview and must be prudent when offering advice that could be construed as influential (American Association for Marriage and Family Therapy, 2001). Therefore, "doing therapy" with family members may be considered by some to be unethical. However, as I mentioned earlier in this chapter, we have a body of knowledge that sometimes lends itself to helping those we love. It is necessary to be mindful of the intent with which we offer help. It seems that if we as therapists keep in mind that we are not doing therapy, but rather are doing what we would normally do if a loved one approached us for help, we are OK. Furthermore, take caution when giving advice (we tend not to give advice to clients, so why would we give it to our family?); as we are all probably aware, advice is rarely accepted in the way it is offered.

Solution-focused techniques seem to be tailor-made for universal use. Nevertheless, as with anything else therapeutic, know what you are doing and where you are going. If your daughter comes home from school one day feeling very sad and you chime in with the miracle question—well, I do not think that that would be very helpful!

A FINAL THOUGHT

My husband and children are not the only family members who are privy to my knowledge of SFBT. To exemplify this, I would like to share another little story. A short time ago, my 80-year-old parents were having some difficulty settling some issues with a vendor. They asked my husband (who is very adept at troubleshooting) to help them out. It took less than half an hour of his time and took a lot of stress off my dad's shoulders. Dad said, "I used to be able to do these things so easily. I don't know why I can't anymore."

I said, "Well, what *were* you able to do?"

He looked at me quizzically, so I elaborated, "What did you do differently today that you might not have done before?"

After a moment he replied, "I asked for help, but it was hard for me to do because I wanted to do it myself."

"Yes," I said. "It's hard, but what came of this hard thing you did, asking for help?"

"Well, I was starting to get stressed and now I didn't have to."

"And," I continued, "when you get stressed, you get palpitations, and when you get palpitations you get nervous that you are having a heart attack again, and because you did something different, you prevented all of that from happening!"

"Yes, Hari," he said, smiling and nodding. With that, my mom looked up, broke into a big grin, and said, "And that…is solution-focused therapy!"

NOTE

1. Credit for the techniques used in this chapter goes to Insoo Kim Berg and Steve de Shazer, whose memories live every time I ask a question!

REFERENCES

American Association for Marriage and Family Therapy. (2001). AAMFT code of ethics. Alexandria, VA: Author.

Berg, I. K., & Miller, S. (1992). *Working with the problem drinker.* New York: W. W. Norton.

De Jong, P., & Berg, I. K. (1998). *Interviewing for solutions.* Pacific Grove, CA: Brooks/Cole.

de Shazer, S. (1988). *Clues: Investigating solutions in brief therapy.* New York: W. W. Norton.

62

INSOO

Jay Trenhaile

I was sitting in a small room with Insoo and Steve and a couple of other trainees in Milwaukee watching a live session on a monitor. I remember thinking, "This has to be the best my professional career can get!"

The second thought I had was about an interaction with Insoo during the SFBTA conference in Park City in 2004. Early one morning, I walked into the fitness room and the first person I saw was Insoo. She had brought a book to give to me. It was as if she knew I would be working out that morning. We visited briefly and continued our workouts. I finished approximately 30 minutes later and Insoo was still going strong.

63

THE DAMN DOG

Thorana S. Nelson

In 1993, the Solution-Focused Brief Therapy Association held its first annual conference, hosted by Loma Linda University in Southern California. Wildfires were rampant before the conference and many people were displaced as they evacuated their homes. The fires were brought under control in time for us to have our conference, but our hotel was inundated with firefighters and displaced people.

One evening, before going out for our festive get-together, my husband used an elevator to go to the floor with the workout room. He is a dog lover and can't resist engaging the little critters. There was a couple in the elevator, apparently some of the displaced people, holding two small show-dog terriers. Vic leaned in to talk with one and the poor creature, already traumatized, I'm sure, responded in a very solution-oriented (to get Vic away from him) way by jumping up and biting Vic in the lip.

Vic and I spent the rest of the evening in an emergency room and roaming for a pharmacy that would take our insurance instead of dining with our friends. The next morning, we met Steve and Insoo in the lobby. Insoo looked at Vic's swollen lip and said, "Victor! I heard you got bitten by a dog!" "No, Insoo," he replied. "I was bitten by a DAMN dog!" Insoo got quite a kick out of that and repeated the story several times during the conference. Vic is more careful around dogs now.

64

A POEM

Dvorah Simon

While I hesitate to "explain" any poem, I would say that this poem and solution-focused brief therapy both participate in the tradition of respecting the silences that join us. Steve de Shazer, in particular, was an artist of silence, completely at ease sitting with a client (or with himself) without the need for words simply to fill the spaces. He taught a way of working in which the therapist, in a certain sense, disappears or is forgotten because what is far more relevant is the client's life, proceeding toward its best unfolding.

1.
You were the unspoken poem.
I drank in your silence,
pacing myself to it,
note by note by note.

2.
This investigation yields nothing but sorrow.
Let us suspend all such endeavors, then,
in favor of the daffodil.

3.
Darling, you have already
forgotten me.
This is exactly
as it should be.

4.
I, too, breathe the wind
inspiriting us both.
There is no need for further
comment.

65

SOLUTION-FOCUSED HAIKUS

Frank Thomas

Editor's note: Introductions for poetry are best left to people like Garrison Keillor. However, haikus exemplify the elegant simplicity of solution-focused brief therapy. The first haiku that follows requires vivid imagination, just like a therapist's task of learning details of miracle pictures. Once found, important details cannot be contained. The second speaks eloquently to one of Steve de Shazer's most amazing skills.

1.
he could not be still
pushed from within, excitement—
urine on my shoes

2.
nothing so sacred
as two humans sharing words
or wordless silence

66

SOLUTION-FOCUSED SONG TITLES

Frank Thomas

Media is endemic in our experiences. It infiltrates our metaphors, our dreams, and our conversations. And music is one of the most powerful forms of media for many people because they can closely identify with lyrics, mood, genre, and even performers. Music can be used thoughtfully to connect, raise a question, or make a point. For example, there are times when a therapist is looking for a way to lighten the moment without losing momentum or creating distance. Humor allows one to say what must be said without the sting of confrontation, and research supports the use of humor in building bonds and normalizing the therapy process. A therapist might refer to a song from this list, using Google to locate the lyrics, and connect with a person whose musical tastes are known through previous conversations.

Here's an example of the use of light humor with a client:

Song: "It Works for Me"—Toby Keith (country)
Therapist: You're a country music fan. Do you know Toby Keith's "It Works for Me"? That's what I'm looking for in all these questions: What works for you?

Music can also expand a concept or normalize a person's experiences. It can be humorous or it can take a serious turn, such as in this example:

Song: "Ordinary Miracle"—Sarah McLachlan (alternative)
Therapist: You're a fan of Sarah McLachlan, aren't you? Me too. Do you know the song "Ordinary Miracle" by her? She sings about

how ordinary miracles are—that miracles aren't exceptional, but that they happen every day for those who hold to their dreams. [The therapist could read some of the lyrics with the client here.] That's what I'm thinking right now…how these exceptions you're experiencing might just be part of that miracle you and I have been talking about since our first session together. What do you think?

Music is a universal language and a powerful way to connect people, ideas, and experiences. Peruse the following titles, check out the lyrics, and see if some of them might be useful to you in future interventions with clients who find meaning, connection, or solace in their music.

"A Couple of Other Questions"—George Carlin (comedy)
"All I Need Is a Miracle"—Paul Young & SAS Band (rock)
"An Exception to the Rule"—Dwight Yoakam (country)
"Asking Questions"—Charlie Wilson (R&B/soul)
"Beginner's Mind"—Old School Freight Train (country)
"Countin' on a Miracle"—Bruce Springsteen (rock)
"Curiosity Song (I Only Want to Know)"—Andrew Gorczyca (rock)
"Don't Ask Me No Questions"—Lynyrd Skynyrd (rock)
"Don't Ever F*****g Question That"—Atmosphere (hip hop/rap)
"Don't Hold Back"—The Sleeping (alternative)
"Do Something"—Macy Gray (pop)
"Do Something Different"—Brave Combo (world)
"Do You Really Want an Answer?"—Zapp (R&B/soul)
"(Such an) Easy Question"—Elvis Presley (rock)
"Easy Task"—Junior Murvin (reggae)
"Ever Hopeful"—Robin O'Herin (blues)
"Fighting Is Not the Solution"—the Mosaic Project (children's)
"Good Question"—Pete Townshend (rock) (album)
"Gotta Question for Ya"—Living Legends (hip hop/rap)
"Honest Questions"—Daniel Bedingfield (rock)
"Hope"—Sublime (alternative)
"Hopeful Again"—Anita Athavale (rock)
"I Don't Know"—Carole King (folk)
"I Found the Answer"—Mahalia Jackson (inspirational)
"I Know There's an Answer"—The Beach Boys (rock)
"If It Works"—Tokyo Police Club (rock)
"In a Win, Win Situation"—Emery (alternative)
"I Need a Miracle"—Grateful Dead (rock)
"It's a Miracle"—Boy George and Culture Club (pop)
"It's Gonna Take a Miracle"—Deniece Williams (pop)

"I've Got a Question"—The Naked Brothers Band (pop)
"It Works for Me"—Toby Keith (country)
"Land of Hope and Dreams"—Bruce Springsteen (rock)
"Less Is More"—Joss Stone (pop)
"Mr. Curiosity"—Jason Mraz (alternative)
"My Conscious Curiosity"—Yesterdays Rising (rock)
"Natural Resources"—Dntel (alternative)
"Never Too Late"—The Answer (rock)
"No Answers Only Questions"—The Alan Parsons Project (rock)
"No Exception"—Enemies (alternative)
"Obvious Question"—Suzanne Vega (rock)
"One Hopeful Day"—Mark Soskin (jazz)
"One Little Miracle"—Hawk Nelson (inspirational)
"Ordinary Miracle"—Sarah McLachlan (alternative)
"Private Conversation"—Lyle Lovett (country)
"Questioning Everything"—8stops7 (rock)
"Questions and Answers"—Rufio (rock)
"Ready for a Miracle"—LeAnn Rimes (country)
"Resilience"—Annabelle Chvostek (folk)
"Salute Your Solution"—the Raconteurs (alternative)
"Same in Any Language"—I Nine (soundtrack)
"Scale Down"—Rising Appalachia (folk)
"Small Exception"—David Ake (jazz)
"So Begins the Task"—Stephen Stills (rock)
"Sometimes Less Is More"—Justin Hayward (rock)
"Starting With a Question"—Jars of Clay (inspirational) (album)
"Stop It"—Rick James (R&B/soul)
"Strength Courage & Wisdom"—India.Arie (R&B/soul)
"The Answer Is Yes"—Javier (R&B/soul)
"The Answer Lies Within"—Dream Theater (rock)
"The Answer to the Question"—Tree 63 (inspirational)
"The Exception"—Eddi Reader (pop)
"The Exception"—Ian McGlynn (alternative)
"The Question Is What Is the Question?"—Scooter (dance)
"There's Hope"—India.Arie (R&B/soul)
"The Scale Song"—Scratch Acid (alternative)
"This Is How It Works"—Lisa Lopes & TLC (soundtrack)
"Unanswered Question"—Amel Larrieux (R&B/soul)
"Verge of a Miracle"—Rich Mullins (inspirational)
"Viva la Resilience"—Turdus Musicus (rock)
"Wait for an Answer"—Heart (rock)
"Waiting for the Miracle"—Leonard Cohen (folk)

"What Works Is"—Tom Russell (folk)
"Wild Hope"—Mandy Moore (pop)
"With One Exception"—David Houston (country)
"You Gave Me the Answer"—Paul McCartney & Wings (rock)

67

FAVORITE QUESTIONS, QUOTES, AND IDEAS[1]

"What's better?"

Solution-focused, not solution-forced. (Nylund & Corsiglia, 1994)

Never work harder than your client.

"What would you like to see different or better as a result of our meeting?"

Words were originally magic. (de Shazer, 1994)

If it works, do more of it; if it doesn't work, try something else.

A tap on the shoulder. (Berg & de Shazer, n.d.)

"What else?"

"WOW!"

"What do you want?"

"What do you do already that works?"

"How do you cope?"

Small changes can make a big difference.

Diagnosis is not destiny.

"How would your best friend know that this meeting/these meetings had been helpful to you? What would you be doing?" (de Shazer, n.d.)

"What would your teachers say you are good at that is not important to you?"

"How did you do that? That couldn't have been easy!"

"What would you have to do to keep doing that; what's working?"

"When they would say you're at X while you say you're at Y, what are they looking at that you aren't? What are you looking at that maybe they aren't?"

"What would have to happen so they might suspect that you might be changing this…at least a little bit?"
"As few sessions as possible and not one more than necessary." (Hoyt, 1996, p. 61)
"What are your best hopes for this session?"

NOTE

1. Contributed by Alison Johnson, Greg Vinnicombe, Tom Lee, and Thorana Nelson.

REFERENCES

Berg, I. K., & de Shazer, S. (n.d.). *A tap on the shoulder: 6 useful questions in building solutions* [CD]. Solution-Focused Brief Therapy Association (http://www.sfbta.org).

de Shazer, S. (n.d.). *"I want to want to…"* [DVD]. Solution-Focused Brief Therapy Association (http://www.sfbta.org).

de Shazer, S. (1994). *Words were originally magic.* New York: Norton.

Hoyt, M. (1996). Solution building and language games: A conversation with Steve de Shazer. In M. F. Hoyt (Ed.), *Constructive therapies 2.* New York: Guilford.

Nylund, D., & Corsiglia, V. (1994). Becoming solution-focused forced in brief therapy: Remembering something important. *Journal of Systemic Therapies, 13,* 5–12.

68

QUOTES THAT SIT WELL WITH SOLUTION-FOCUSED APPROACHES[1]

If, at first, the idea is not absurd, then there is no hope for it.

—Albert Einstein

We can't solve problems by using the same kind of thinking we used when we created them.

—Albert Einstein

All evolution in thought and conduct must at first appear as heresy and misconduct.

—George Bernard Shaw

Each problem that I solved became a rule which served afterwards to solve other problems.

—René Descartes

When you can't solve the problem, manage it.

—Robert H. Schuller

Never bring the problem solving stage into the decision making stage. Otherwise, you surrender yourself to the problem rather than the solution.

—Robert H. Schuller

No problem can withstand the assault of sustained thinking.

—Voltaire

It's so much easier to suggest solutions when you don't know too much about the problem.

—Malcolm S. Forbes

Most people spend more time and energy going around problems than in trying to solve them.

—Henry Ford

To every problem there is already a solution whether you know it or not.

—Grenville Kleiser

To solve the problems of today, we must focus on tomorrow.

—Erik Nupponen

There are no problems, only solutions.

—John Lennon

If you see your path laid out in front of you—Step one, Step two, Step three—you only know one thing…it is not your path. Your path is created in the moment of action. If you can see it laid out in front of you, you can be sure it is someone else's path. That is why you see it so clearly.

—Joseph Campbell

As a grown man you should know better than to go around advising people.

—Bertolt Brecht

We do not see things as they are. We see them as we are.

—The *Talmud*

Things are not as they seem; nor are they otherwise.

—Lankavatra Sutra (Zen koan)

Since all the world is but a story, it were well for thee to buy the more enduring story than the story that is less enduring.

—St. Columba of Scotland (Cade, B., & O'Hanlon, W. H., 1993. *A brief guide to brief therapy.* **New York: Norton, p. 109)**

NOTE

1. Contributed by Paul Hanton, Netti Kutsche-Roth, and Alasdair MacDonald.

V

Outrageous Moments in Therapy

While gathering material for this book, some of the people on the SFT-l Solution-Focused Listserv that is managed by Harry Korman (www.sikt.nu) started talking about things that they had done in therapy that were rather embarrassing. Regardless, these are accomplished therapists and either their faux pas had no deleterious effect on therapy or clients, or they were able to turn things around. These are pretty funny, but a standard caution applies: *Don't try this at home!*

69

AN UNUSUAL AND TRUE ANSWER
TO THE MIRACLE QUESTION

Jeff Chang

I was seeing a woman who was expressing dissatisfaction about the loss of passion in her marriage and the lack of connection with her husband. After I asked her the miracle question, she said, "Well, I'd wake up and I'd be in bed with my husband, and I'd kiss him, and maybe, you know, we'd get into it a bit. And I'd get kind of turned on and then maybe I'd, well, I'd give him a blow job."

Being a very well-trained solution-focused therapist, I had a number of almost automatic responses at the ready. But as I did a mental search of my possible responses I had to eliminate all my well-programmed responses:

- Let's say you did that, what would he notice? *NO*
- So what would that look like? *NO*
- How do you think he would respond? *NO*
- As you were doing that how would he be feeling? *NO*
- What would you be saying to yourself? *NO*
- What would happen next? *NO*
- If he did _____ how would you respond? *NO*
- Then what? *NO*

It seemed like I sat there for about half an hour doing a mental search for an appropriate answer. It was probably more like 10 seconds. Much to my relief, I finally said, "So, after you were all done, how would that help the day get off on the right foot?" *PHEW*

70

LIAR, LIAR

Phillip B. Ziegler

Early in my professional career, I was clinical director of a community counseling agency where we provided free family therapy to adolescents and their families. I saw a teenage girl who was referred by her high school because she was caught drinking with some friends on campus. We met and after hearing from her that her father was a serious drinker, we invited her entire family to come in for a session.

The girl brought her mom, dad, and sister into the session. In my efforts to welcome the dad and make him comfortable, I asked what kind of work he did and he explained that he was a lineman for the phone company. Before we could go much further, the dad said he was concerned about both of his daughters' drinking. The mother and the two girls didn't say much at that point. After listening to his concerns, I tried to shift the topic from the girl's drinking to the general theme of alcohol use and possible abuse in this family.

Now the mom and the two girls began talking about the dad's drinking. He would have none of it and wanted to go back and talk about his daughters' drinking. He denied that he was a heavy drinker and, given his angry tone of voice, it wasn't surprising that the other family members backed off. I could see that the wife and kids were afraid to say more and it got really quiet in the room. I was not sure whether to "challenge the denial" or back off and take the pressure off the dad so as not to lose his participation.

As I was trying to figure out what the master family therapists would do, all of a sudden, much to my own surprise, I turned to the dad, pointed my finger at him, and blurted out, "Liar, liar, pants on fire. Underpants hanging on the telephone wire." Everyone in the family laughed, including the dad. I was shocked, but the family's response allowed me to recover my composure. The dad then announced that he knew it was time, if he wanted his kids not to drink, he would have to deal with his own drinking. And we went from there. When we came to the end of our work together, the dad said he knew in that first session that, "You really knew what you were doing and I knew you could help me and my family." Go figure.

71

F**K-OFF THERAPY

Dvorah Simon

It occurs to me that some clients want and/or need "empathy" more than others. Some would like someone to problem solve with them, stay on task, and be reasonable and polite. Others find solace in a shared expression of feeling. Others like plenty of mirroring (behaving in ways and gestures similar to the client's) and others couldn't care less. Some like their emotional tone to be matched and others seem to like the injection of humor to lighten things up or otherwise shift things.

My very first client after internship, years before I got my PhD, was a woman, "Joan." She was small, wiry, dressed in jeans and jeans jacket, with short hair in a masculine style. On our first meeting, Joan thrust out her hand to shake mine and said, "My name is Joan; they call me the dyke with the spike."

Joan told me her story in hints and generalities over the next few weeks. I had the sense that, as with her initial introduction, she was testing to see if she could spook me. I must have looked young and soft—I was certainly new to therapy and had not even heard of solution-focused therapy at that point. If I can imagine back, I think my idea about therapy was to provide a safe, welcoming environment in which Joan could share what she needed to, but not to do anything more directive or focused.

One day I was wearing a jacket my mother had sent me in the mail. It was a bit unusual—short, almost bolero style, in a silvery quilted fabric. Joan started to tease me about the jacket. "What kind of stupid thing is that? It's so short it won't cover your butt, won't keep you warm; what's the point?"

Her teasing pushed a button. I said, "Hey, my mother gave me this, stop criticizing it." This was said in a somewhat teasing tone back, in a similar New York street style that Joan used. Joan took this as license to continue mocking my jacket, of course. I protested and she continued.

Finally, in a moment of pique, I blurted out, "Aw, f**k off." I was shocked at what had come out of my mouth! You don't tell clients to f**k off!!! How unprofessional! How rude! I couldn't believe what had happened.

There was a stunned silence. Joan and I stared at each other for what seemed like an eternity. Finally she started laughing, HARD. She laughed so hard she was shaking and slapping her thighs. Every time she tried to settle down and say something, she'd look at me and start laughing again. I was in my chair, saying, "What? What's so funny?"

When her giggle fit stopped, many minutes later, Joan looked at me solemnly and said, "NOW I know I can trust you. If you can talk to me like that, I know you're strong enough to hear the things I need to tell you."

After that, she opened up about a world of abuse—sexual and physical, being forcibly institutionalized by her family for being lesbian, years of drug and alcohol abuse. We worked together for about 2 years, at which point Joan got into her first relationship in 14 years. She found another kindred soul to share her life with.

Moral of this story: It's a terrible, wrong, bad, rude, unprofessional thing to do to tell a client to "f**k off"…except when it's exactly the right thing to do.

72

T-SHIRT

Paul Hackett

A young lad came with his dad to see me. The dad said his son would not speak to me and then we proceeded to have a great session with son involved. At the end, sneakily fishing for compliments on my own brilliance, I asked how come the son had decided to talk today. Dad answered in a flash, "It's because you are wearing a t-shirt."

73

OVER-DEVELOPED EMOTIONS

Chris Iveson

A couple of evenings before this therapy session, we'd had some friends round for dinner. One of the friends and Di, my wife, were talking about how easily they both cried and, firstly, how embarrassing it could be, and, secondly, how it could escalate the apparent seriousness of a situation when the tears suddenly came in the middle of an argument. Di coined the "diagnosis" of *over-developed emotions,* or ODE.

The client had come because of a life-long diagnosis of depression that she described as constant worrying, distress, and tearfulness.

I said, "You've got the same problem as my wife but possibly a more serious case of it!"

"Oh! What is it?" she said, for the first time with interest and animation in her voice.

After a pause and a sigh, I told her straight: "It's ODE and it's a tough one to deal with."

A look of such relief came over her face. "So you know all about it?" she asked.

"Yes," I replied, "I certainly do."

"That's what I want!" she cried. "An expert!"

After giving her my diagnosis of ODE, we had two more sessions and stopped after she had experienced "tears of joy" at her daughter's wedding.

74

OUTRAGEOUS MOMENTS IN THERAPY

Paul Hanton

MISJUDGEMENT

A young man who was quite severely depressed and very frightened to go out and be "around people" was making some great strides in getting better. So I asked him what would be the best he could hope for if he was really, really better. He replied that he would love to go and watch his local football (soccer) team play, but the crowd of 12,000–15,000 was too scary. This team had been relegated from the English Premier Division, down to the next division, so I said, "Mmmmm, so you want to go and see Barnsley play? No wonder you're depressed!"

This was of course meant to be funny and lighten the mood. He looked at me with a stony expression that told me I had misjudged things somewhat.

HOT POTATO

I was working with a woman who cared full time for a relative with congenital heart failure. She told me that if she could just walk across some fields and hills without feeling guilty for taking time for herself, she would feel much better. Even though the person she cared for encouraged her to take this time, she felt she couldn't as guilt was like a "hot potato." Taking a lead from her, I suggested a between-session task of going for said walk, but before she went she was to microwave a potato, wrap it in tin foil and when she was walking and felt guilty, she was to throw the hot potato away. She did this and reported that she had looked around to see if anyone was watching her throw this hot potato as she felt so stupid doing it. She carried on walking after that, laughing to herself.

ASSERTIVENESS

Recently I saw a woman who was "suffering" from "low self-esteem" and "lack of assertiveness" (words used by her referring general practitioner). During the course of our first meeting, she asked me if I had any children because we were discussing the fact that her children had grown up and moved away. I told her, "Yes, I have a 13-year-old and a 23-year-old." She replied, "Oh, you don't look bad for your age then."

My response, after a brief pause, was: "Now we've got the assertiveness sorted, what else shall we work on?"

She laughed somewhat, as did I, and it is fair to say a rapid therapeutic alliance was evident and I went on to look for more exceptions to her "lack of assertiveness" and "low self-esteem."

FROM THE FLOOR

A young drug user had been to three sessions. At each one, his sum total responses were "yes," "no," or "don't know." He could not answer a best-hopes question (What are your best hopes for this session?), scaling seemed impossible, and whenever I tried to engage him in problem free talk, he simply lowered his head and pulled his baseball cap farther down. I decided that something had to break this pattern, so I asked him to look at me because I could not tell whether he was interested in what I was saying or not because I could not see his facial expressions. He pulled the cap even lower.

Why I did what I did I still don't know, but I got on the floor and lay at his feet so I could see his face and said, "That's better." He laughed and said, "You're f***ing mental." From that point on (after I got back in my seat), things were a little easier. Apparently he told some of his friends what I had done and they found it very amusing—unlike some professionals I discussed it with who "told me off" because he could have kicked me in the face. But he didn't!

GETTING CLOSE

A woman had been referred for therapy due to fear of having an epileptic fit. Her last one had been 5 years previous to our meeting. When asked about how her partner of 10 years would notice she was getting better, she replied, "I don't know, because we are not that close; maybe I'd 'let him in more' to my thoughts." I commented that as she had two young children, I guessed that they had been close once. Her reply: "Not really. Well, sex gives us something to do when we are bored."

FIRST SIGN

After asking a young man the miracle question, very carefully and with some seriousness (I had just watched a de Shazer tape), I asked, "And what would be the very first sign that things were getting better?" His reply: "You would stop f***ing patronising me!" I apologised and moved swiftly on.

NO ONE LEFT

An administrator once told me a young man had arrived for his first session with parents, grandparents, and siblings in tow. She said, "I wouldn't bother. He has said he does not want to see you." I opened the door to the room he and his family were in and said, "I understand you do not want to see me. You know where the exit is" and left them for a few minutes. No one left. I returned to the room and said, "Hi, I understand you want to see me."

CHILDISH

I have to confess that I have never told a client to f**k off, though I did say to one, not so long ago, "Stop being so childish," when she stamped her feet while telling me, "You're the therapist; it's your job to sort me out!" I was mortified—It just came out. I took this to supervision, fully expecting the client to make a complaint. My supervisor was pretty cool and told me to wait and see and we would deal with it if and when.... When this client arrived for our next meeting, she was completely different and said to me that it was about time she grew up and dealt with her s**t. She had gone from 0 to 6 on her scale. Oh well....

VI

Resources

75

SOLUTION-FOCUSED QUOTES

Steve de Shazer was a contributor on the SFT-l Listserv that is managed by Harry Korman. Some of the nuggets he contributed follow (his comments are in italics).

1. In a message dated 10/30/00 8:12:53 PM Central Standard Time, ziegler@IGC.ORG writes: << therapists don't need to actively work on relationship factors. >>
   In a good SFBT interview, the interview does the job—without any extra burden of "working on building rapport/relationship"— the client too is automatically doing the same job without trying, it happens. Of course in a less good interview...the compliments at the end, if well done, can keep things going.

2. In a message dated 10/31/00 7:21:50 AM Central Standard Time, ziegler@IGC.ORG writes: << In workshops participants often express doubt about how rapport can be built asking sft questions. >>
   Tue, 31 Oct 2000 09:05:12 EST. *More importantly, rapport can be maintained through good SFBT interviewing.*

3. In a message dated 3/28/01 9:23:33 AM Central Standard Time, WalterPeller@AOL.COM writes: << Today, I would use the language of conversation and for me that allows me to think that the relationship is defined from within and, as you say, that the relationship and the activity of the session are not separate.>>
   Wed, 28 Mar 2001 15:10:23 EST. *Well, as I see it, if two (or more) people are having a conversation, they cannot not have*

a relationship. Now, whether it is a "good" one or not is another question. But I am mainly interested in whether or not it is "useful" to the client and thus I continue to use the "techniques" (questions, wow, etc.) that we have long found useful. Thus our work together stands a good chance of being useful to the client. It seems to me that it is almost as if the client comes in open and ready for a useful relationship and all we really have to do is make sure that we do not undermine or destroy it.

4. Wed, 21 Mar 2001 23:49:23 EST. *While clients are experts in their lives, therapists need to be experts in doing therapy. Hopefully, both experts learn something over time and when the therapist knows something because he's an expert, then he should let the client know. As Brian Cade has said, he's an expert on things that do not work.*

OTHER CONTRIBUTIONS

Too often people who want to learn SFBT fall into the trap of not being able to see that the difficulty is to stay on the surface when the temptation to look behind and beneath is at its strongest. (Correspondence with Steve de Shazer, September 5, 2001) In Lee, M. Y., Sebold, J., & Uken, A. (2003). *Solution-focused treatment of domestic violence offenders.* New York: Oxford University Press, p. 18.

—Contributed by Lorenn Walker

All that is necessary is that the person involved in a troublesome situation does something different.

—Contributed by Alasdair Macdonald (de Shazer, S., 1985, *Keys to solutions in brief therapy.* New York: Norton. p. 7)

At the Narrative Therapy Conference in Reston, VA, some years ago, someone asked Steve about working with at-risk kids. Steve pulled on his beard for awhile, and then said, "I think we're all at risk, all the time!"

—Contributed by Arnold Woodruff

The version I heard about this was at a conference (not clear what kind of conference and not clear when), the experts are supposed to say something in the panel about teenagers at risk. Steve is the last one to take the microphone and he says, "We are at risk from the day we are born till the day we die" and then he sat down again.

—**Contributed by Harry Korman**

An attendee at one of Steve's events queried if the SF approach was "too superficial" and Steve replied, "I hope it's not as deep as that"!

—**Contributed by Greg Vinnicombe**

From Insoo: There is no such thing as multiproblem families, only multiple goal families.

—**Contributed by Harry Korman**

Insoo: We'll come back to that [and then she does not].

—**Contributed by Alasdair Macdonald**

Insoo: I like working with recidivists. They are really good at making fresh starts.

—**Contributed by John Wheeler**

As few sessions as possible, and not even one more than necessary.

—**Contributed by Thorana Nelson (Foreword in Dolan, Y., 1992, *Resolving sexual abuse: Solution-focused therapy and Ericksonian hypnosis for adult survivors*. New York: Norton, pp. ix–x)**

There are cases in which you can do the whole therapy without needing to know what the problem or complaint is.

—**Contributed by Thorana Nelson (S. de Shazer in Cade, B. W., 1985, The *Wizard of Oz* approach to brief family therapy: An interview with Steve de Shazer. *Australian and New Zealand Journal of Family Therapy*, 6, 95–97, p. 96.)**

The death of resistance.

—**Contributed by Thorana Nelson (de Shazer, S., 1984, The death of resistance. *Family Process*, 23, 79–93.)**

Where you stand determines what you see and what you do not see; it determines also the angle you see it from; a change in where you stand changes everything.

—Contributed by Thorana Nelson (de Shazer, S., 1991, *Putting difference to work*. New York: Norton, p. xx)

76

CONTRIBUTIONS OF STEVE DE SHAZER
(1940–2005) TO BRIEF FAMILY THERAPY

Janet Campbell

Steve de Shazer wrote five books as a single author and coauthored several others. He published 55 single-authored articles and coauthored 42 others. He described his work as "rooted in a tradition that starts with Milton H. Erickson and flows through Gregory Bateson and the group of therapists-thinkers at MRI." He described himself as a "technician," a "voice of the chorus," helping to clarify and organize the ideas of other therapists, his own ideas, and descriptions of his own work and that of other core members of the Brief Family Therapy Center (BFTC) of Milwaukee, Wisconsin. The BFTC team included, at different times, Insoo Kim Berg, Marvin Weiner, Elam Nunnally, Eve Lipchik, Alex Molnar, Marilyn Bonjean, Wally Gingerich, John Walter, Michele Weiner-Davis, Jim Derks, Marilyn LaCourt, Ron Kral, Kate Kowalski, Scott Miller, and Gale Miller. There may be others that I have unintentionally omitted.

The following are the books solely authored by Steve de Shazer and some of the contributions of each.

PATTERNS OF BRIEF FAMILY THERAPY: AN ECOSYSTEMIC
APPROACH (1982) NEW YORK: GUILFORD

Use of direct observation: viewing and reviewing
John Weakland (in foreword): "No written account of therapy can fully substitute for direct observation (as is true for the

transmission and learning of any craft)" (p. vi). Direct observation describes the work of Steve with the team at BFTC. By
having the apparatus available, they could watch a large number of family sessions and could therefore see patterns.

*"Resistance" replaced by "client/ family's unique way of cooperat-
ing" (p. 9)*

BFTC's work used a particular team approach. They began
using a consulting break as part of the session. Then, participants behind the mirror became part of the "therapy
team" instead of being separate from the therapy. The
"compliment" as part of the team's feedback to clients was
developed during the break as well as a task. There was an
element of "resistance" idea. This was redefined as the cli-
ent/family's unique way of attempting to cooperate.

No grand theory: tasks are related to response to previous task

The team developed a "step-by-step" approach tailored to the
particular family. This forwarded the idea of no grand theory. BFTC developed a method of relating one task to the
response the family reported to the previous task.

KEYS TO SOLUTION IN BRIEF THERAPY
(1985) NEW YORK: NORTON

Focus on solutions rather than on the problem

Steve de Shazer: "After 15 years of doing and studying brief
therapy I have come to...[the] conclusion that forms the
central premise of this book. For an intervention to successfully fit, it is not necessary to have detailed knowledge
of the complaint. All that is necessary in a troublesome situation is that the person involved *does something different*"
(p. 7).

Set up conditions for spontaneous change

It became clear that the goal of therapy was not "elimination of
the symptom" but helping the client set up conditions that
allow for spontaneous achievement of the goal.

Small changes lead to other changes

By 1979, a new perspective was developing. de Shazer became
more and more convinced that clients really do want
to change. "The key my colleagues and I invented for

promoting cooperation is quite simple: *First we connect the present to the future (ignoring the past), then we compliment the clients on what they are already doing that is useful and/ or good for them, and then—once they know we are on their side—we can make a suggestion for something new that they might do which is, or at least might be, good for them*" (p. 15). "Only a small change is necessary as it can lead to other changes. Therefore only a small and reasonable goal is necessary" (p. 16).

CLUES: INVESTIGATING SOLUTIONS IN BRIEF THERAPY (1988) NEW YORK: NORTON

Change happens before therapy begins

Previously, therapeutic change was seen as primarily related to tasks and clients' reports of homework performance. Here, there was more focus on solution-related things that the client and therapist do during the session. One project (Weiner-Davis, de Shazer, & Gingerich, 1987) looked at "pre-therapy change" based on two first sessions where clients spontaneously mentioned a change had happened prior to the session. From the beginning of the first session, therapist and client are constructing a therapeutic reality based on continuing transformation or change (as evidenced by any exceptions) rather than on initiating change.

Skeleton keys

This book explored the idea of skeleton keys: tasks transferable from one client to another that are useful in opening the door to change in many situations. For example, "Observe, so you can describe to us next time, what happens in your family that you want to continue" (p. 2)—that is, a skeleton key for searching for exceptions that could be made into differences that make a difference.

Miracle question

Used consistently in the first session to elicit concrete and specific descriptions of what the goal will look like.

PUTTING DIFFERENCE TO WORK
(1991) NEW YORK: GUILFORD

Therapy as a negotiated, cooperative endeavor with the aim of constructing solutions

Helm Stierlin (foreword): "Steve de Shazer make[s] his case for therapy as a 'negotiated, consensual, and cooperative endeavor in which the solution-focused therapist and client jointly produce various language games focused on a) exceptions, b) goals and c) solutions'" (p. 74; p. vi).

Steve de Shazer: "This book will focus on critical readings that, to me, seem to be useful in thinking about what it is that is going on in the clinical situation and in *seeing* what happens in therapy" (p. xviii).

From book jacket: "Steve de Shazer...situates the solution-oriented model within the developing purview of post-structural thought....Therapy becomes conceptualized as a conversation in which the therapist and client work together—through language—to construct solutions." Causality is seen as useless to the conceptualization and practice of therapy.

WORDS WERE ORIGINALLY MAGIC
(1994) NEW YORK: NORTON

When we take clients' words at face value, we realize how clever clients are

This book explores how Steve de Shazer tried to find out the theory that could be used to understand Erickson's work. It seemed that, no matter what was tried, there were always oddball, miscellaneous cases that didn't fit—formerly attributed to Erickson's idiosyncratic genius. de Shazer began to wonder if he'd been missing the point all along. Maybe there was nothing hidden away at all and variety and diversity were the essence of Erickson's approach—as if there were many branches but no center whatsoever; no grand design, but instead local activities that were situationally dependent. He re-read Erickson's case examples using a reading strategy that involved taking words at face value, keeping his reading on the surface, avoiding reading between or behind or beneath the lines. He found the client's characters were under-realized. Then he re-read his own cases from this point of view and came to realize what clever clients he had.

Client's goals—client's solutions

Brian Cade (on book's jacket): "In *Words Were Originally Magic,* Steve de Shazer considers language and discourse, and challenges us to bring more rigor to the frequently vague and nonspecific debate on therapy as conversation, as a process of 'co-creation.'...Here he is concerned with the assumptions and the kinds of conversation that respectfully and economically facilitate clients rapidly discovering *their own* solutions and achieving *their own* goals....Continually highlighted is the importance of looking at the actual words used by the clients and by the therapist, and at the pragmatic effects of these utterances."

REFERENCE

Weiner-Davis, M., de Shazer, S., & Gingerich, W. J. (1987). Using pretreatment change to construct a therapeutic solution: An exploratory study. *Journal of Martial and Family Therapy, 13*, 359–363.

NAME INDEX

SUBJECT INDEX